ONLY THE DEAD CAN KILL

Stories From Jail

MARGO PERIN

Contributing Editor

In Collaboration with COMMUNITY WORKS/WEST

Foreword by Ruth Morgan

COMMUNITY WORKS/WEST
Berkeley, California

For permissions contact: info@communityworkswest.org

Published by Community Works/West
1605 Bonita Avenue
Berkeley, CA 94709

Interior artwork by Michael Francis

Cover art by Jan Freeman Long, www.janfreemanlong.com

Cover and book design by Jan Camp, www.jcampstudio.com

Printed in the United States of America

ISBN: 0-9779741-0-3

1 2 3 4 5 6 7 8 9 UNITED 10 09 08 07 06

To the men and women and boys and girls incarcerated
in the thousands of jails and prisons spread across
the United States. Tell your stories.

ONLY THE DEAD
CAN KILL

CONTENTS

Contents

197 Dress Outs

FOREWORD

The publication of *Only the Dead Can Kill* marks the end of a unique sixteen-month collaboration between Community Works/West and writer-teacher Margo Perin. For the past twenty years, Community Works has been dedicated to using the arts and education as a catalyst for change among underserved populations in the San Francisco Bay Area, including incarcerated offenders and ex-offenders living in the community. Our mission is shaped by a strong belief in restorative justice, a criminal justice model in which offenders, by exploring how they have been both victims and perpetrators of violence, come to understand how their crimes have deeply impacted themselves, their families, and their communities.

The jail arts programs has become an integral part of the Sheriff Department's commitment to the re-education and rehabilitation of offenders. They are the heart and soul of the jail programs giving offenders new tools and creative space to explore themselves. The writings in this anthology, raw and highly personal, represent a powerful step in a much longer restorative journey that begins in the unlikely setting of a jail.

Only the Dead Can Kill is a rare multimedia collaboration between an accomplished writer, Margo Perin, and adult inmates in San Francisco County Jail. Over a yearlong series of narrative-writing workshops, Perin guided a group of male and female offenders through a process of exploring their lives through narrative. Above all, it was her own courage in sharing her story of being raised by a criminal father that inspired the inmates to write about their experiences with such unflinching candor. In dedicating themselves to this project, these remarkable authors made a commitment to transform their suffering and perpetration of violence into creative writing that is both profoundly personal and courageously public. Reading their stories, we see and understand what joins us as human beings. As Perin says, it was her intention "to break through the inevitable isolation that crime brings and to forge connections through artistic collaboration with the wider society." We present this material in book, audio, and online formats to enable it to reach beyond the classroom and touch inmates, their families, and communities near and far. It is our hope, at this time of great disappointment and grief following the very recent execution of Stanley "Tookie" Williams, that this moving work created by incarcerated men and women will demonstrate the possibility we have to change and grow, to take responsibility, to mourn, and to mend. The publication of *Only the Dead Can Kill* is one step in a long process of personal healing, accountability, and community restoration. We hope, too, that it can mark one more step toward the goal of convincing our society that a truly "just" criminal justice system can and should have rehabilitation as a core value.

There are so many who made this project possible. First I want to thank Margo Perin for her deep commitment to her students and this project. It has been a joy from beginning to end to collaborate on all aspects of the development of *Only the Dead Can Kill* and we are so proud of the book produced out of the project.

Tremendous thanks to Francis Phillips and the Creative Work Fund for their generous support of this work. Their continued commitment to and their belief in the power of the arts to strengthen our communities has enabled the creation of extraordinary new art works in the counties of San Francisco and Alameda for a dozen years.

Of course I want to thank Sheriff Michael Hennessey for his continuing dedication to arts and education programs in the jails and his absolute belief in rehabilitation of those in his care; we appreciate how extremely important the commitment to rehabilitation is for prisoners, their families, and our community as a whole. A very special thanks to Sunny Schwartz, Program Administrator for the Sheriff's Department, who has been responsible for so many of the visionary programs in our county jail and who continues to be an inspiration to all of us in this work. I also must acknowledge and thank former San Francisco Assistant Sheriff, Michael Marcum, though retired now, it was his commitment to and vision of *what is possible*, that changed the face of the San Francisco Sheriff's Department forever and made programming of this depth possible.

Thanks to Albert B. Waters II, Chief Deputy of the San Francisco Sheriff's Department and to Floyd Johnson and the staff of county jails #7 and #8 for their work. Much much appreciation to Leslie Levitas for her enthusiasm and tremendous support of all of Community Works' programming for over a decade. Equal thanks to Delia Ginorio for her continued support and belief in the power of the arts to transform lives.

Tremendous gratitude to Jan Camp, for turning the manuscript into this beautiful book; to Ellie Erickson, for all her critical administrative work, good humor, and amazing overall competence, and to Samantha Morgan, for proofing and other work on this project.

Above all I want to thank the writers who have so generously shared their stories with us. We at Community Works hope that the experience of *Only the Dead Can Kill* has been as meaningful and enlightening and empowering for them as we believe reading the important and moving work that has come out of the project will be for our communities.

— Ruth Morgan
Director, Community Works/West
Winter 2005

PREFACE

Only the Dead Can Kill is the result of a collaborative project between Community Works, people who are incarcerated at San Francisco County Jail, and myself to shed light on the life experiences of people who live behind the walls. This book and CD were inspired by my creative-writing teaching at the jail, as well as my experiences with my father's criminality. Through the generous funding of the Creative Work Fund, men and women at the county jail and I have been able to give voice to our experiences in this public forum. It is our hope that our voices will speak to the larger community and encourage a process of healing and restorative justice.

When I began teaching at San Francisco County Jail four years ago, I didn't think I had anything in common with my students. I felt compelled to teach in jail, for reasons yet unknown to me, but I was so nervous about being locked up with criminals that as I drove up to the gates on my first day, I found I was driving on the wrong side of the road. A deputy in a white van swerved past me, shaking his head as though I was already in trouble. And, in a sense, I was. Little did I know how many of my own buried feelings and experiences would come to the surface behind those fortified walls.

I knew that when I was a child my father had committed crime, but he didn't go to prison. Many people commit crimes, especially white-collar crimes, and get off scot-free. He disappeared often, he did have a bodyguard, and he did come home with black eyes, and later black thumbs, and later still after having all the bones in his face broken, but my father never went to prison. Therefore, I had the luxury of ignorance about who and what lay on the other side of the thick walls that section off large portions of the population from the rest of us, and the luxury of ignorance about how much emotional terrain I shared with my soon-to-be students.

When I began to hear the stories of the men and women who volunteered for my classes, my experiences were spoken to in a very direct way, giving voice to feelings that had never found common ground with my supposed peers. My students had been victimized, abandoned, and traumatized, and they needed to heal. In a very different way, I had been victimized, abandoned, and traumatized, and I needed to heal. My students oftentimes had turned to drugs as an attempt to keep their pain at bay; in my life, cancer and other illnesses had kept the wolf at my door. As has been said, if crime is the wound, then healing is the justice, and that was the road that my students and I embarked upon, leading to this collection of autobiographical stories and poems.

The production of this collection by my students and myself created a community of experience, crossing borders of race, gender, class, and sexual orientation, and allowed us to swim together in the same river of humanity. Our work has been profoundly transformative, acting like alchemy; as it illuminated what lies in the shadows in the lives of my students, it shed light on my own experience. It has helped us understand more about who we are behind the definitions others have made of us, and who we are in our own right, separate from the people in our lives and their stories.

The concept behind the title *Only the Dead Can Kill* is that only when people are shut off from their own humanity are they able to dehumanize themselves and others. This is true for people on both sides of the criminal fence. Criminals are commonly dehumanized and vilified by a public that turns its back on the causes of crime. Those of us not caught up in the criminal justice system, and supposedly protected from those who live behind the walls, commonly relegate these men and women to a darkness that, metaphorically, holds our own shadows. When we don't look at people behind bars as human beings with relationships, with hopes and aspirations, or connected to families or communities, we don't have to look into our own wounds, or face the ways in which all our lives are interconnected.

We have a tendency in the United States to oversimplify and only think in the short term: a crime is committed (those that are prosecuted) and the perpetrators (mostly poor and disenfranchised) must be punished. We don't think about what it does to someone who is already very wounded to be wounded more by the dehumanization of incarceration, nor, more important, do we think about the historical or socioeconomic realities of most people who end up in jail. Perhaps that is why we make people invisible and don't treat them as human beings: because it is too painful to see how our realities intersperse with theirs. We don't see that what we have relates to what others don't have, and we don't recognize the direct link, in our iniquitous society, between how our inability to create safety and protection for all of us affects our individual safety. We don't see that we all, from cradle to grave, have the same needs. We also don't see that treating people as inhuman can become a self-fulfilling prophecy.

One day in the cavernous, dimly lit warehouse scantly populated with tables and chairs that served as our classroom, a group of formally dressed civilians stood at the mouth of the room and looked in without addressing my students or myself.

"Who are they?" one of my students asked. When I shrugged, his friend said, "They come and look at us like we're animals." He opened his mouth wide and roared like a lion. I laughed, but his point didn't escape me. If we are raised with no expectations, undervalued, and given little opportunity for growth and betterment, then almost inevitably we become what is expected of us.

When we don't tell the truth about our lives, whenever we dehumanize, objectify, "invisibilize," as it were, our own feelings and realities, we, in a sense, "kill" ourselves. When we don't face our own wounds and attempt to heal them, when we don't tell what happened to us or reveal our true thoughts and feelings, we kill who we really are. We are not living our lives, but instead the lives that we perceive others have constructed for us, whether those others are family members, community leaders, or society as a whole. And, in so doing, we also kill our ability to perceive the humanity of others. We become both the killers *and* the killed. By moving in the opposite direction and attempting to understand the people we fear, we get to understand the parts of ourselves that we fear. This allows us to not only make connections with each other, but it also brings the strength and courage to live our lives more fully and positively.

Writing or speaking our stories from our point of view is what allows us to become the authors of our own lives, rather than victims of the definitions that others have made of us. When we tell our stories and express our hurt, we learn to tolerate our pain. We lose the need to hurt others, or hurt ourselves because we believe we deserve no better. In other words, we bring ourselves back to life.

People who commit crimes are often not just perpetrators, but also the victims of crime themselves, whether those crimes are social, economic, familial, or personal. They are rarely given the opportunity of a good education, therapy, or the social and economic support to heal and reverse this victimization. Their wounds often xiv

remain invisible to others. As a result, these children, as youth and adults, become involved in a cycle of violence and abuse in which they themselves go on to become perpetrators of crime. In place of receiving recognition and help to heal the wounds, they act out from those wounds.

Quite aside from serious familial abuse, which is frequent, the poverty and violent conditions in which millions of Americans are forced to live as children, and do not have the resources to escape as adults, create a culture of brutality in which people who are abused hurt others because that is what they know.* You could say that these men and women were "good children" because they learned to cope by adopting behavior that they needed to survive in an inhumane world. Out of necessity, they shut themselves down to assuage their pain, and as a result, they became cut off from their humanity. They lost their ability to empathize not only with others, but also with themselves. What is tragic is that these "good children," as adults, often end up being destructive, to themselves and others, and we can see the results of that in the crimes that are committed. I'm not speaking of crimes of drug use or drug sales, largely resulting from the so-called war on drugs which has replaced programs to end poverty, but crimes in which people are violated: robberies, rapes, and killings, crimes that themselves are often drug related.

In a weekly writers' group setting of a year, as well as by mail upon release or transfer to other jails and prisons, men and women who are incarcerated wrote their life stories, artistically exploring the sources and ramifications of crime in their lives, as well as the effects on their families and the community. At the same time, I wrote about my own experiences.

Some of the men and women you will find in these pages came to the writing class because they liked to write. Others came because they wanted something to do. One writer told me that, starved of contact with women, the men were signing up because a woman was teaching the class. In the women's jail, some of the writers, most of whom suffered even lower expectations of themselves than did

---

* Not everyone in the pages of this collection comes from a poor, urban background. Interestingly, most of those contributors with greater social advantage are former foster or adopted children who suffer the lifelong pain and emotional dislocation of abandonment. KPFA recently reported that 70 percent of prisoners at San Quentin State Prison are former foster children.

the men, came simply to hang out with their friends, or because they heard I was handing out notebooks and pencils. But once they were there, we got serious.

The first assignment was to write one's life story in twenty minutes. "Any time you want to put in a period, put in a comma," I instructed, "and don't change anything. Just write." What I wanted from them was one long run-on sentence, to free them up from the self-imprisonment of criticism and censorship. That way the experiences that were most important to the writer would come to the surface.

When they were finished, the writers read out their stories, and then I gave individualized assignments based on what they had written, focusing on where the heat was in their writing. As they continued to write, I encouraged them to go deeper into their emotions. "How did that make you feel?" I constantly asked, pushing them to go behind the masks of their own protection. I tried to follow my own advice, asked them to give me assignments, and shared my stories with them.

My own personal story is about invisibility and the search for identity and a sense of home. When I was seven years old, my father, who had been jailed several times, received word he was about to be investigated for his participation in an investment heist. My parents, siblings, and I began a life on the run so he wouldn't have to serve a twenty-year prison sentence. In seven years, we covered five countries and two continents. By the time we reached London, England, our last port of call, my father had changed our last name and our distinguishing details of ethnicity, family, and history. I learned that we came from nowhere, and I grew up defined by what I was not, rather than by what I was.

As I embarked on this project, I thought if I could figure out what my father had done, I would be able to fit together all the puzzle pieces of who I was. But as I continued to write, I realized that what was important were not the details of my father's story, but the details of mine. I discovered that the point was my own healing, just as my students' telling their stories from their point of view became a way for them to begin to heal from their own victimization.

The journey that took place as the people behind the walls and I gave voice to our narratives is illustrated by the stories and poems you will find within. Every one of the 2.5 million Americans who are currently incarcerated might be sectioned off to where it is dark and where others cannot see them, but they are there. If the world listens carefully, they will be heard. And as this happens, we can all become more closely attuned to our own stories and develop the fortitude to be the creators of our own lives. We hope that our writings will encourage you to walk into your own shadows and tell your stories.

To maintain the authenticity of the writers' voices, the stories and poems appear as they were written, with only minor editing of punctuation, spelling, and paragraphing to make for easier reading, and with the occasional change of wording for clarity. A handful of pieces were excerpted for reasons of space.

My deepest thanks to the writers in this collection for all that you shared in the creation of this project, and for the generosity of the Creative Work Fund and the collaboration of Community Works for making this project possible. Heartfelt thanks to Ruth Morgan for her vision and her dedication to providing excellent arts programs at the jail and for all her support and belief in my work; and to Frances Phillips for her support and encouragement. Thank you to Sheriff Michael Hennessey for his foresight in bringing arts programming to San Francisco County Jail and to Sunny Schwartz for her work in making it possible. A special thank you to Leslie Levitas for creating the first bridge, and for her continued support. A big thanks to Jan Camp for her superior design. Thank you to Samantha Morgan and Ellie Erickson for their excellent typing and hard work, and to Jeanne Halpern, Stephanie Losee, Jesse Obstbaum, Audrey Ray, and Joey Scuderi for their artistry and support.

My gratitude for your healing, illumination, and inspiration: Valerie Mejer, Denise Douieb, Rosemary Rau Levine, Karen Nani Apana, Pamela Lewis, Sharon Hennessey, DP, VP, LP, Marci Klane, Teresa Camozzi, Lisa Kellman, Dino Lucas, Jennifer Gordon, and Gordon Smyth.

— Margo Perin
Winter 2005

Life Story

My name is . . .
My name is . . .
My name is . . .
Please show me the name Inmate on a birth certificate . . .
—R. L. Love

DWIGHT YOUNG

Déjà Vu

February 7, 1979
My mother gave birth to a set of twins
We were created out of an act of lust, not love
To survive in this world of sin
Moms was incarcerated at the time she had us
Newborn infants
Opening our eyes as wards of the state
Little bitty shackles
With orange jumpsuits
Yet to suffer the ultimate fate
Mama checked out on life early on
Left me and my brothers to fend for our own
The trials and trivialation and obstacles of life
Them storms is what nursed us and made us strong
I've walked in the shadows in the valleys of death
I fear no evil, evil feared me
It actually was the light
I chose to walk in
Because in my troublesome times
God's footprints was still next to me
The day came when I thought I could walk on my own
And I turned my back on my God
I spun around and what was staring at me

I fear no evil, evil feared me

A sentence of thirty-one years to life
I stopped and thought to myself
Déjà vu
Is this the beginning of the end?
And then I remembered
This is exactly how the beginning for me
Beginned!

回

ROGER HAZELETT

What You Think I Am

What you think I am
Is not who I am
For if I am who you think I am
Then I am a man who loves life
I am a man who has caused pain
I am a man that has taken a life
I am a man that is full of pain and shame
I am not who you think I am
I am what I didn't want to become

I am not who you think I am / I am what I didn't want to become

回

DAVID GARNER

Life Story

I was born March 26, 1977, in San Jose. I don't know if my father was there. I know that I grew up in a house with Moms.

My father was a man that was in the army. I had my mother and a dog and me.

I really can't remember too much about my life. I was in a private school that I didn't want to be in. I was a troubled child. I liked to play without any work. I was told as a child that I couldn't play if I didn't do any homework. Sometimes I had to be disciplined. Sometimes it was on my knees like an airplane, saying, Mommy, Daddy, can I get off these knees, please?

I used to get beat with cords and sticks. Sometimes I even had to sit and soak in the bath from Dad whipping my ass. How long will this last before I can kick his ass? Now I'm close to seven. I called on heaven. Then it came to me that I'm going to call my aunt before I'm whipped to death. I'm already whipped until I bleed, almost losing my teeth. Man, I'm calling my auntie, come free me from this man-beating machine.

Through this time of coming up I had to take care of and help my mother with my two little brothers. We started going to church with my aunt. I think that Sunday school was the best and safest place for me and my brothers.

Now I'm getting older. I'm back in school in the sixth, seventh, and eighth grade. I'm about to go to the ninth grade, which is in Walnut Creek. My mother moved around a lot. I've always had a problem with making friends. Well, in this city was where I took off. The ninth grade was fine. This was the year that I got into trouble with the law for stealing. My mother was at home. Well, anyways, I wanted to be cool and go out and get what I wanted by stealing. So while I was doing this, I ended up getting into trouble.

I never really wanted to stay at home. It wasn't like the *Bill Cosby Show*. I really didn't have a father at home to talk to. I always wanted to be the man of the house, without any income. Even though Mom was sending me with her money to pay the bills. So I thought I was the main man. When Mom got a boyfriend the man of the house's role was stripped from me. So I went to the streets. I didn't want to be chastised by anyone that wasn't my blood. So I ran away from home.

While I was on the street I started to drink alcohol more. I was a hurt little boy that only wanted to spend time with his father. I have always wanted my dad to find me. I really wanted to be with my father. All I wanted to know was how to live life, and I wanted it from his lips. Not from another man. So I was alone.

So while I was in the street my drinking and stealing put me in jail for a month. I was in there for stealing. I couldn't call my mom. The police didn't want me to go home. So I told them I had a drug problem with weed and alcohol. They told me that this addiction starts in the house. So I went to a program so that I could stop the path that was self-destructive within myself.

Well, I ended up going to a drug program. The program I went to was in Oakland. I went there for a year. I finished the program and wanted to go home. I couldn't go home because of my mom's old man. So I went into a foster home with one of my brothers from the program. I went to this house in Concord off Clayton Road. I had two lesbian parents that really liked and loved me. I went there very scared and didn't know what to expect.

I really wanted to be with my father.

回

DEBORAH WALTON WITH DALE WALTON

Then Comes Rain . . .

May 3, 1985
A dope fiend was born
Molestation by Daddy
Eyes full of scorn
Innocence was taken
Mommy called the cops
CPS takes three children
But the cycle don't stop
Blinded by pain
Rebellion and hate
Got adopted at six
It happened

**ONLY THE DEAD
CAN KILL**

Too late
Grew up with a fire
That no one could tame
Yeah, some days were
Sunny . . .
But then came the rain
Now they tell me I'm
Pretty . . .
My sex appeal shows
Inside I hate sex
But I hide it
No one knows
I feel overrated
My outside ain't
Shit
Compared to my mental
But they all want to hit
Why no one asks questions
Does no one really care?
There's more to me than
Pussy, pretty eyes, and lustrous
Hair
Intellectually splendid, more
Caring than most
Talented and funny
Mind expanded
God's the host
I once was truly happy
Thought my life would
Soon change
The sun peeked out for
A second
But then came the
Rain.

KRISTIAN MARINE

White Boy in an Asian Body

I was born somewhere in Seoul, South Korea, on November 28, 1976. Surnamed Kwon, meaning power or authority, and given the name Myung Sung, meaning future success. Nothing in any of the circumstances surrounding my birth suggested fulfillment of such an auspicious name. Soon after I took my first breaths of life, I was housed in an orphanage with countless other infants awaiting an unsure fate. Without even saying so, Korean culture's weighty emphasis on bloodline widely discouraged adoption. Most orphans, therefore, would grow to become tolerated, though generally disdained blemishes in the Korean social fabric, having no provable lineage or genealogy. As I lay there fidgeting and crying, I had no idea that my life would take me halfway around the globe, where I would grow to understand who I really am.

Thousands of miles from Seoul, in a small Norwegian town in northeastern Iowa, lived Konrad and Kay Marine. Konrad, the only orthodontist in Decorah and the surrounding towns, was enjoying early success as the owner of two busy practices. Kay carried a light workload as an administrator at a nearby college in order to spend time caring for their two three-year-old children. Three years earlier, while living in Panama, this young couple had discovered they could not biologically have children. It was a difficult reality for them to face. After some serious thought, they decided they would adopt children and, soon after, they were the proud parents of a beautiful baby girl. Kara Kay Marine was born of a Panamanian aboriginal girl of the Cuna tribe and left on a doorstep in the wealthiest district of Panama City. With no birth records accompanying her, her date of birth was designated May 16, 1973. Months later, Konrad returned from San Jose, Costa Rica, with a malnourished baby born May 25, 1973. He was later named Kirkland Konrad Marine. The little family was growing.

Konrad, Kay, and the two Ks, as they affectionately referred to their little ones, returned to the United States. They settled in Decorah, Iowa, where they had met as college students several years earlier. Konrad bought the practice of a retiring orthodontist. Kay found work at Luther College, and their life took off. Diligence and strict financial responsibility—two prominent characteristics of my father—led to the young family's monetary success, stability, and abundance. With an already comfortable lifestyle and sufficient resources, they started thinking about adding some more Ks.

This time they chose to work through an adoption agency in St. Paul, Minnesota. The agent they consulted with was a young Korean woman who knew about a large number of Korean orphans who needed good homes. Pictures of the newborns were posted on the wall of the agency and, after some serious consideration, Konrad and Kay selected two—a boy named Kwon Myung Sung and a girl Kim In He. At that time there was a limit to the number of internationally born children a family could adopt. Konrad and Kay worked diligently with their state representative and congressman and ultimately obtained two documents signed by President Jimmy Carter to allow the adoption of the two infants.

We arrived on December 7, 1977, fat cheeks, thick yellow baby outfits with fake Mickey Mouse logos, and all. We were greeted hesitantly by our four-year-old siblings. Pictures of our arrival show them with bewildered expressions. Konrad and Kay were all smiles, though. We were the new center of attention and would remain the center of our parents' attention as we grew, much to the continued bewilderment of Kara and Kirk. We were taken to our new home, far from the familiar faces, voices, and aromas of Seoul, and given the new names Kristian Kwon and Kaili Kim.

Decorah was a good place to grow up. It was a small, safe community where children were allowed to roam around unattended. Among my earliest memories are summers filled with explorations in the woods on paths cut by curious children long before me. My home at 719 Ridge Road was situated at the border of the woods. The quiet, never-ending expanse of hills, trees, and valleys with ruins of old forts and hideouts created a magical world far from a sometimes turbulent home life. Just standing in the woods hearing the wind rustle through the green canopy high above and seeing bright beams of sunlight break through to the forest floor seemed like a heavenly experience. There was an electricity that ran through me when I contemplated the incredible beauty of nature. This same feeling still occurs within me today.

My childhood was also filled with friends, picnics at the park, and thrilling Christmases of Transformers, cars, and video games. And, like all children, I also had a fair share of bumps and bruises. Early one summer afternoon, I returned with Mom and Kirk from the bike shop where Kirk's bike had just been repaired. Mom popped the trunk and went in the house, leaving us in the garage to get the bike out. Being five at the time, I was not very coordinated. As we worked together to lift the bike from the trunk of Mom's little maroon Dodge Omni, my left hand slipped off the tire and my left pinky was thrown in between the sprocket and chain. One of the teeth of the sprocket was driven through the top joint of the finger. Without stopping to assess the situation, I started yanking wildly to get my finger out. After a few desperate tries, I succeeded in freeing myself from the sprocket, only to discover the top third of my pinky was missing. As my eyes relayed the shocking message to my brain, I did the only sensible thing a five-year-old would do—I stood there and screamed. Two fountains of blood sprayed forth from the mutilated nub into the trunk of Mom's car. The top third of finger lay on the garage floor, propelled from the bike by the force of the separation. Kirk stood in front of me in wide-eyed horror. Fortunately, my panicked screaming reached Mom's ears and she came running to my rescue. A quick car ride to the hospital, a short surgery, some stitches, and a candy bar later, things were pretty much back to normal—all except the missing digit.

My childhood accidents and injuries kept me in touch with my mortality and helped me understand myself on a human level.

*"Nigger?" I thought.
My reaction was a
mixture of hilarious
disbelief and hurt.
I was pretty sure
that I wasn't one.
I mean, I didn't
think I was.*

Children are resilient and generally bounce back from these experiences. But the experiences of discovering who I was—my personal identity—have really shaped the man I am today. Those experiences began in Decorah, too. I came to understand myself in the context of my community. The beginning of this awakening is illustrated in an interaction on a playground when I was eight years old.

"You . . . you . . . you nigger!" he sneered at me.

"Nigger?" I thought. My reaction was a mixture of hilarious disbelief and hurt. I was pretty sure that I wasn't one. I mean, I didn't think I was. "That's just black people, isn't it?" I thought to myself.

I wanted to laugh but the humor quickly turned to anger inside me. Whether I was a nigger or not wasn't the point. He was trying to hurt me and I knew it. Mrs. Hulk, my third-grade teacher, and the rest of the recess duties had already filed in through the doors of the red-brick school. My classmates, in the safety of the classroom, were already returning their jackets to their coat hooks, designated by name stickers, and were getting ready for class, oblivious to my plight. Three of us stood at the far end of the asphalt playground in the sea of small rocks that housed the tall metal swing set. I knew there was nothing I could do. Danny Pitts, the class bully, stood there looking down at me threateningly in his dirty green jacket and red freckled face. His eyes were cold and mean, daring me to do something. Larry, his nerdy sidekick, stood just to the right of Danny, glaring through thick glasses. To my surprise, neither of them made any threatening advances. After all, maybe this nigger knew karate or something. No words were exchanged, and after a moment of thick, angry silence, we all just started walking toward the door of our classroom at John Cline Elementary School. It was a sour ending to a gray day of recess, and no one, not Mrs. Hulk or my parents, would ever know about that day on the playground.

Thinking back, I can't remember what immediately preceded that confrontation or what made Danny call me that name. I seem to remember pushing Larry off the swing or something. That's not the point, though. Even the name he called me is of little consequence to me now. It is the deeper meaning behind the name that keeps this memory etched in my mind. It told me that I was different.

Growing up in an all-white community, I inwardly became a reflection of what I saw. When I say all-white community, I mean I can only remember seeing ten non-Caucasian people in that town (three of whom were my siblings). As a child looking out of my body and not at it, I failed to internalize my physical difference from those around me. I often forgot I was Korean—jet black hair, the shape of my eyes the subject of children's jokes. But that autumn day on the playground, I awoke to a realization that I was different, and the white boy in my Asian body could never change that. I felt helpless and hurt.

I was just as good as other kids. It wasn't my fault that I looked different from them. I was white, too! Everything about me said that—my speech, my tastes—everything but my body. And that is what people saw. They saw a gook, a chink, or "were you that Chinese kid in that movie?" I was constantly asked about martial arts and Asian languages, neither of which were part of the culture I was familiar with. So who could I identify with?

Since the Asian community in the Midwest is basically non-existent, I continued trying to be accepted by the larger white community, the same community that enjoyed making fun of people that looked like me. The resulting loss and confusion from this social amputation was greater than the simple loss of a finger ever could be. Didn't Jesus say, Fear not that which kills the body but that which kills the soul?

No help from Mom, surgery, or candy bar could help with this.

*the only thing that /
Mattered to me was
me . . . and that's
the story of my life.*

BRYAN TROSCLAIR

Life Story

Why can't I elude
The troubles of these ghetto streets . . .
My anger started when
Death claimed the life of my only friend.
Herb the only friend I ever had lost
His life to the streets and when the Creator
Called for him back I didn't know what
To do. My sane world had ended at the
Age of twenty-two. I shut my heart down
And held my bitter pains in.
       Introverted and a lover I
Soon became and the only thing that
Mattered to me was me . . . and that's the story of my life.

回

ZAKIYA CRAIG

Life Story

Hi, my name is Zakiya Craig. My name means the intelligent,
wise one. I'm an only child. Both of my parents are still living.
My mom was a single parent. I went to a lot of elementary schools.
My mom's mom was abusive to me. She used to beat me. I went to
private school. I got good grades. But had bad behavioral grades.
I do believe it was because of my abuse and being the only child.
Always feeling alone.

   After my grandma beat me into a blackout, I moved in with my
grandma on my dad's side. She tried to keep me active in ballet,
dance, and sororities. Then later I was able to move back with my
mom.

*Always feeling
alone.*

My mom never opened her feelings up to me. She never taught me how to be a woman or about periods or what kind of guys to choose in life. I felt unloved at fifteen. Had a baby when I was eighteen. I was in an abusive relationship from the age of fifteen to eighteen. I stabbed my firstborn's dad in the head out of self-defense. I went to jail for attempted murder but got released in two weeks because it was self-defense.

My dad used to feel on me. He would always try to keep me locked up. He had me sent to the Huckleberry House. He would cause me to run away. Then I moved in with my mom.

I left my mom's house when I was nineteen. I found my own place to stay. I started selling drugs downtown in the Tenderloin. I stopped at the age of twenty-three. I started to date my husband at nineteen. He helped me change my life. I had another baby at twenty-one. We got married November 9, 1999. We were together for eleven years. He was a sweet, strong, charming, protective man. He would go back and forward to prison, so I would find myself working or hustling in the neighborhood I grew up in.

I've seen a lot of people getting killed from the age of fifteen until now. I'm twenty-seven. My husband got killed in front of me last year, three days after Christmas, on December 28, 2004. He was my love and life. I saw him get shot. They tried to kill both of us when we were coming out of the house. My husband let them shoot him so they wouldn't harm me. He died in my arms. I came to jail after I buried him. I miss him so much. Now I'm in jail full of pain, anxiety. I have two beautiful kids that I love so so much. They're all I have in life now besides the Lord. They are very unique children. I'm upset at myself for having a nervous break-down and allowing myself to be selfish and inconsiderate and come to jail. Not realizing that they needed me, just lost their dad and now their mom is in jail. Now I'm realizing I need my kids bad.

My husband got killed in front of me

Roger Hazelett

Life Story

My name is Roger. I am the youngest of 12 children. I was born in St. Helens, Oregon. When I was 6 we moved to Portland. I was not allowed to go to school with my brother so I ran the streets. A special lady talked me into going into the army. I spent the next 3 years in Vietnam. After I came home I got into trouble and spent the next 12 years in the state pen. I am now looking at 25 to life.

I have traveled from Portland to Salt Lake City, 972 miles. I have been to Washington, DC, another 2,122 and back 4,244. I have traveled to Vietnam 3 times, 14,288 miles, not counting the ones I walked or crawled. This is not counting the miles of tears that I have caused or cried. But I've come to see the longest distance is from my heart—18 inches. Why does it take so long to go so short a distance?

I was in a physical prison for 15 years. All I saw was cold, gray walls. Day in and day out around the track I walked. There are 3,500 cracks in it. Then I hear the loudspeaker saying, "Yard in"; back to the 8 x 12 I call my house. Breakfast is at 4:30 AM. Then it's either work line or yard line. I would hear people say I will soon be free. But that's just another word to me. "Freedom is just another word for nothing left to lose." The day came when they said I was free. What they did not know is that I had built a prison inside of me.

The day came when they said I was free. What they did not know is that I had built a prison inside of me.

Chaz Long

Life Story

It was the year of 1984 when I was born in San Francisco at Children's Hospital. I was the first child of my twenty year old mother and the youngest of my father's seven kids. In my infant and toddler years I never really seen my father because he went to the penitentiary for ten years for a major drug bust. My grandmother and great-grandmother were like my mom in those years because my mom was working two jobs to take care of us. I ended up starting preschool when I was four years old and was at the top of my class so I was skipped through kindergarten straight to the first grade. I pretty much ran through elementary school going to E. R. Taylor in the San Bruno area of San Francisco.

By the time I graduated from elementary school my father was just then getting out of the pen and my mother had another son on the way. It was the summer going to sixth grade when I really knew who my dad was and I began learning the streets through him. He was a big cocaine dealer and was a huge factor in the Fillmore area. It was the time for sixth grade now and I still wasn't infatuated with my father's lifestyle. I was a straight-A student and loved school and basketball.

Through my junior high school years I still stayed with Mom but was being raised by Great-grandma. I was the star point guard on the basketball team and graduated with a 3.83 GPA. It was summer after eighth grade and by this time my father was back on track with his cocaine business, giving me a three hundred dollar allowance and I'm only thirteen. Now was when I started getting infatuated with this lifestyle, so much money at such a young age. I wanted to be just like him and my mother seen that and she started keeping me away. At the same time she's trying to keep me away, I'm sneaking to go see him. I liked the money and the things I could buy with it. Growing up in the projects of Hunters Point you didn't see little kids with $150 tennis shoes and Nintendos, so I was happy.

It's time for high school now and even though I was starting to be infatuated with my father's lifestyle, I liked the attention of playing basketball and having As more than anything. So I went through high school doing my thing and graduated at the top of

I was a straight-A student and loved school and basketball.

*It's hard for a black
kid in that area to
ever see twenty-five.*

my class. I had went down south to tour colleges and ended up at Dillard College to get my business license. I let my basketball dream go and spent my time getting my business license. Once that was complete, I ended up in San Francisco at a loss with myself, meaning I didn't know what to do next. I found myself back in the projects with my father, seeing him still getting money and at the same time as there's money there is a turf war in my area and you're pretty much guilty by association. And being back in the neighborhood put me in the position to carry a concealed weapon. My dad gave me seven thousand dollars to put into a foreclosure to start my laundromat business but at the same time I'm living in the projects carrying a weapon. Then one night walking to the store, not on probation even, or parole, I was jacked by undercover police because, as they say, everybody in a predominantly black neighborhood looks suspicious, and here I am today.

My projects are called Harbor Road, better known as Big Block in the Bayview Hunters Point area of San Francisco. There are about five different projects in the Hunters Point area and there is a war going on between them. Since about the early 1990s the war has been going on, nothing changes, people die and people are raised to hate the other projects. The Hunters Point area is 85 percent African American and 50 percent drug addicts. The rest of the other young African Americans are drug pushers/killers. Everybody carries a weapon, kids stop going to school after eighth grade, and they feel the only way of life is to slang drugs. And that's all they see. It's hard for a black kid in that area to ever see twenty-five. Last year there were about forty to fifty murders in that area alone, and 80 percent unsolved.

Life Story

I am an American of Persian descent. I was to be raised in Iran by my paternal grandparents but my mother (blonde-haired, blue-eyed, "legs up to there," user of wealthy Middle Eastern men) fought him in civil court over me. I was pawned as having material value to her—and she had me reared by her Polish-Lithuanian parents in Pittsburgh, PA, and I haven't been the same since!

I don't think most people really know what to make of me. By all appearances I seem to be a privileged intelligent lady of European descent until my name is seen or heard. All Persians know my name is of Middle Eastern descent so that seemingly always opens one of many dusty, rickety Pandora's boxes strewn throughout my divine chaotic existence.

I was born in Georgetown, Washington, DC. I've always declared that my home. I've been in San Francisco for roughly six years and still exclaim that "I'm just visiting!" I excelled in school as a gifted student until I got bored with most educational instruction in the ninth grade and would run away from home once spring bloomed in the air. Returning in tears with my tail 'twixt and 'tween my legs, to return home to the cold dampness of early fall only to find out I received an incomplete for ninth grade and had to repeat the school year. I repeated the same exact cycle that same school year. (By seventh grade I was, upon my insistence, living with my mom—a single mom with overabundant support from my father—in the Washington, DC area.) So upon entry for the third time to give ninth grade another chance, I gasped at the pint-sized peers in class next to my 5'10" shapely postpubescent torso-bearing hips and I just walked away and promptly and successfully received my GED and never looked back. However, I couldn't wait to go to college so I applied and was accepted into the local community college taking courses in everything that either (a) sounded of interest to me, or (b) perhaps would improve my beingness into a Renaissance,

By all appearances I seem to be a privileged intelligent lady of European descent until my name is seen or heard.

self-styled young lady. Over an eighteen month time frame I took Intro to AC/DC Circuitry (Electronics), Computer Programming (FORTRAN/Algorithims), Commercial Design, Voice and Diction, English Composition, and Intro to Logic (this being the only class that I failed miserably, and in humiliation I still nowadays, in jest, say this failure is the bane of my existence which explains my lack of common sense).

回

MICHAEL FRANCIS

Footprints

I had a dream I lived a life in the manner of men.
It was filled with the pleasures and pain I thought was the norm
for one who lived rebelliously in this day and age.
Suffering and strife littered the path of my own choosing.
I never felt extraordinary in the least, yet
knew normalcy was not in my makeup.
I cared not whether I fit in and knew instinctively
I was the proverbial round peg in this world
of square holes and cared not for others' opinion
    in this matter.
I feared no man, for I knew I, too,
held the potential and power over another's life and death,
same as any other man who recognized no man's
boundaries and respected only as I chose.
I lived the "high life" and in the depths of poverty
and was a true survivor. The mantle fit my shoulders the same,
no matter the situation. Then this dream turned to nightmare.
I recall, as I tread this path, I looked over my shoulder down
    this road I had walked and I came to the realization
that no matter how hard my feet had pounded through this life,
I had left no footprints.

no matter how hard my feet had pounded through this life, / I had left no footprints.

CHRISTINA PASSMORE

Life Story

My name is Christina Marie Passmore. I was born November 3, 1972, in Tacoma, Washington. I was adopted three months later, as my birth mom was young and overwhelmed with the burden of raising an infant.

I lived in the same house for nineteen years. My parents never moved.

I have one brother. He is four years older than I. His name is Robert and he is a successful professional who travels abroad seventy percent of the year because he loves travel and being single. He is based out of Portland, Oregon.

Upon graduation from high school I took some college classes, but felt a strong urge to free myself from organized academics. Therefore I finished one semester of local college and moved on. I wed a Green Beret from Fort Lewis, moved to Monterey, California, then Honolulu. We were together five years, then I left to return to Seattle. Our separation was due to his military missions, which tore us apart. We divorced soon after my move back home to Seattle.

I lived the wild single life for a good year or so in Seattle. I dated a Russian international business transactions attorney, an airline pilot, an MD who specialized in homeopathic medicine, and a guitarist in a local band. The doctor had the biggest influence incidentally as far as career direction. I studied medical assistanting at the American College of Medical Education.

I worked at Overlake Hospital in Bellevue, Washington after my externship, and as usual decided the medical profession wasn't for me. So I quit my job and started looking for a new one. Anton Lyapin (the Russian) moved back to Moscow to work for a French law firm. He proposed before he left. I declined.

I lived in the same house for nineteen years. My parents never moved.

I came across another lawyer. He is also a writer. We clicked immediately and I worked for him up until a year ago. The other three boyfriends I mentioned faded out as my friendship and work for Joel took charge.

It's ironic that on the big screen criminals and prisoners are often glamorized—gutsier, slyer, and more fascinating overall than the average square. In reality, however, although these traits remain, society doesn't appreciate them as they do in movies.

To quote Chekhov from "A Boring Story" wherein an aging professor of science cites his chief and fundamental fact of existence as insomnia, and to add an emotional dimension to my life story in fifteen minutes, here is my reply and conclusion: if I were asked what is now the chief and fundamental fact of my existence, I would reply, Grit to the core and compassionate karma. After almost three weeks straight of inmate food, I'm uncertain if the grit I refer to isn't a hot cereal.

Dylan M.

Life Story

My given name is David M. I was born in the month of September, on the twenty-third day in 1974 at Palm Hospital in Garden Grove, California, where my mother, as a young single mother in the seventies, strove for wide open spaces and liberalism. These wide open spaces led my mother and I down the galloping path of smoking pot together and attending many rock 'n' roll concerts and gatherings. At these gatherings I was introduced to a lifestyle of sex, drugs, and rock 'n' roll. With this rock 'n' roll I seen my mother raped and beaten at the young age of five years old.

But not all this rock 'n' roll was bad. I can remember many late nights of laughter and dancing. During much of this laughter and dancing I can remember taking shotgun hits of pot from my cousin

Denise and family, enjoying myself very much. When the adults would get together I would always anticipate a good party. My mother would try and have children's movies for us kids there, a cluster of about two young boys my age and four girls a bit older in age. We had fun together. Falling into younger roles of our parents, we were like midget adults. The movies never lasted, with the roar of music and people talking and yellin' all through the house. So of course we kids always joined in duplicating what our parents did, at least to the best of our ability. I always had a good time with the girls.

None of this, however, prepared me for grade school. I was lost and alone. My beliefs and practices had no bearing here. I can remember the first and second grades and even kindergarten feeling humiliated and lost. My pot smoking in the morning left me burned out by noon. I was useless. I tried not smoking but couldn't handle the social tensions. I can remember being called up to the chalkboard in the third grade feeling terrible not knowing the answers. I tried to study but was just too far behind. The schoolteacher always just passed me from grade to grade.

As the years progressed and I grew older in years and strengths, I too became a young parent like my mom, with much different views though, and better beliefs due to my stepdad's influence. So at the young age of fourteen and a half my girlfriend and I sought out to have a child to start our own family and traditions. This means of escape for me was to get away from my mother. At the time she was getting out of prison and I just couldn't live with her and my stepdad at the same time. So within a year of my fifteenth birthday, my bride-to-be gave birth to my son, Dylan Jr. This was the most incredible event in my life, witnessing this new life, this gift of God. I was awe-stricken, full of much zeal and motivation to raise this child with much more detail to attention than my mother. I was so proud and full of life, eager to show everyone I could do it and beyond.

The remarkable thing was, I did. My son was reading and writing before his time. The practice of consistency my stepfather displayed

we were like midget adults.

and taught me paid off. It was as if everything I touched prospered. I soon became involved with helping other young parents in my church life as well. This was all very exciting. For the first time in my life, people needed me. My stepdad, Tom, taught me so much responsibility, I was like a machine, anything that came up at work or at home I could handle with maturity beyond my years. I was promoted at work every quarter. My son was the greatest motivation for me.

So while all this was going on ten years had passed before I could catch my breath, though now I had three additions to my family and was married. And with this third wind I owned my own roofing business and was involved with many other church projects. My family was full of passion. It seemed nothing would stop me.

As I look back, some years have passed since those family days. Because, yes, I was stopped, maybe it was my pride and hopes that led to such a great fall. Today I'm divorced, the papers were signed in 2001, by 2002 I lost my children. This loss was due to anger and bitterness toward my wife and eventually myself. I wish I could say drugs were my fall in all this; however I was clean at the time for almost ten years. However, now I'm an addict and a felon. This is still not acceptable to me. But still I must go on in heaven or earth, I still must go on. I'm tired, I just want to have my family.

PATRICIA ROBINSON

Life Story

I was born in Cleveland, Ohio, and I lived at 1450 East 510 Street with Mr. and Mrs. Peterson. They died and I went upstate and spent the rest of my childhood with Roosevelt and Birdie Marie Latimore. Was finally moved to 38 b4 East 155 Street. And I went to John F. Kennedy Junior High. I went to TRI-C, a community college, and then to Antioch College.

I had a nervous breakdown and returned to Cleveland. In the end Mommy nursed me back to good health. Afterwards I started looking for my biological family from the East Coast, the South, the Northwest, and California. I met a lot of great people.

回

TIMOTHY HECK

Life Story

I have a medical condition that causes my colon to grow to abnormal sizes. I've had this condition my whole life. It's not as bad now as it was then. I can't eat high-sugared cereals, red meat, bananas, or apples because of it. When I follow my diet, I use the restroom about twice a month.

When I was a kid I didn't know about this, and neither did my parents. So there was nothing stopping me from eating all the apples I could find. The effects didn't take place until a couple of days later.

First there's this mild discomfort around my kidneys, then I start to sweat profusely. The pain increases and sitting becomes uncomfortable. Even standing becomes impossible after awhile. Thankfully the pain doesn't last that long, it just kind of comes and goes.

Apples and bananas work as a natural laxative, but for me they don't. When I was a kid, I had a bowel movement once a month if that. Sometimes after using the restroom my hands would shake from the pain. I can't imagine giving birth to be much different.

Large amounts of sugar gives me the runs. So certain holidays like Christmas and Halloween caused lots of embarrassing moments when found too far from a toilet. Can you imagine the amount of

The world so freely shared its pain with me, and I shared mine with no one.

shame involved, and how much pride you have to swallow? To tell your parents that you shit yourself again at school? Considering the violent way that they dealt with everything?

My mom thought I was too stupid or lazy to go to the bathroom. I didn't know what to tell her. I mean, never once was this considered a medical issue.

In order to save myself a whole bunch of humiliation, I started to throw away my underwear whenever I had an "accident" so that no one would know. It didn't take long before all my clothes started to smell.

The ridicule that I endured at school is what the Bible describes as hell. Kids can be so cruel. No matter where I sat in school or in class, I was always within earshot of somebody's insulting remarks. During lunch I would walk around the outskirts of the playground, while the kids threw rocks.

It was only a matter of time before my mom noticed the missing clothes. My disorder had started to become a financial burden for her. Also having to call the plumber all the time cost money she didn't have.

My mom became physically violent towards me. I felt so alone, and cried myself to sleep every night. The world so freely shared its pain with me, and I shared mine with no one.

Late one afternoon, my mom found a pair of soiled underwear in the trash. She chased me into the bathroom and began to beat me. She then began to rub the dirty underwear all over my face and then beat me harder.

When it was all over, I just lay there crying. I've never cried so hard before in all my life. I started to throw up 'cause it was in my mouth and ears, nose and hair. It was everywhere and I was covered in it.

She said if I wanted to act like a baby, she would treat me like one. She went to the store and bought the biggest diapers she could find. She told me that if I didn't wear them she would beat me.

I gave into fear and did as I was told. I'll never forget how the next day at school went. My brother told his friends and his friends told their friends, and so on, and so on.

I was surrounded during the lunch break. Somebody came from behind me and pulled my pants down. I don't know how to describe to you my humiliation. I pulled my pants back up and looked around to see who saw. Everybody was staring back, laughing. I ran and hid in a bathroom stall until school let out.

Somebody later suggested to my mom that she take me to see a doctor. I was then referred to a specialist named Dr. Shinkein. That's when the truth came out.

My mom said she was sorry for the misunderstanding. Her apology fell on deaf ears. I was already cold and bitter. The doctor went on to say that my disorder had progressed to an uncurable stage. It could have been stopped had they caught it sooner.

If I don't keep a close eye on my diet, my colon could rupture and I'll die. Knowing this has helped taint my outlook on life.

I was prescribed all kinds of medications. High-fiber drinks, syrups, and pills. This is how I found out that I have a bad gag reflex.

I was supposed to take these two pills three times a day. They were no bigger than a coated aspirin, but to me they were huge. I barely gagged on the first one, the second one came back up in a pool of blood. My mom picked it up off the floor and pushed it back down my throat. The spit and blood helped it go down. No matter how much she beat me, I would not be doing that again.

After my treatment began I was taken to the hospital for some tests. I was injected with three gallons of this clear oil-looking fluid that was fed through a tube stuffed up my nose, leading down to my stomach. It took three nurses and two doctors to hold me down.

Every time I threw up, it was measured and replaced. There was some talk about inflating a balloon in my colon to find out how big it had gotten. I wasn't about to let that happen. Cable TV and the food was good. I was there for ten days.

The pain and ridicule that I experienced through all those years has left me with a profound understanding of just how ugly people can be. I was just a kid and already full of more pain and fear than

*Something died on
Something died on
those tracks, and it
wasn't me.*

I knew how to handle. Fourteen years old, I couldn't take it any longer. Every traumatizing moment of my childhood contributed to a suicidal attempt in its own little way. It was nothing bloody or gory, but profound to me nonetheless.

I was near some train tracks when I made a decision. I found a nice quiet spot to lay my neck across the track and let the train do all the work. While staring at the sky, my mind began to drift. I saw images and reenactments of the moments that brought me to this crossroad.

I could see all the kids pointing and laughing, but I couldn't hear them. I just watched as the image slowly faded away.

I also saw my mom's face as clearly as if she was really there. It was twisted in anger, but I wasn't afraid. I knew I didn't have to be afraid anymore, 'cause it was all over. That image also faded away . . .

That's when it hit me, it really was all over, and I wasn't afraid! One deep breath, and a wave of goose bumps that wouldn't go away for a long, long time. I was free.

I found where my pain ended and I began. Something died on those tracks, and it wasn't me.

FRANCIS SMITH

Life Story

*Some of these
things I considered
normal behavior, a
way of life.*

My name is Francis Smith. I was born in Buffalo, New York on May 20, 1969. I am the youngest of three and have one brother and one sister. My mother left my father. At the time I was two years old. We moved out west. She didn't know anyone and had no education. She soon became addicted to drugs and my sister, my brother and myself were exposed to the many dark behaviors perpetrated by addicts and alcoholics. I was beaten and molested and grew up very confused and feeling unloved. Some of these things I considered normal behavior, a way of life.

I learned at an early age how to survive on the streets and picked up some very useful though highly negative skills for doing so because I wanted to be loved and I learned that when I had money I had friends so I learned how to make money fast.

At the age of twelve I got into heavy drugs such as cocaine, crack, speed, acid, and PCP. I was only emulating those whom I looked up to—my elder peers and idols. Since I caught my first felony at eleven years of age, I was brought into the penal system early. At that age it was not punishment to me. I really enjoyed it. I had lots of friends and a warm place to sleep and was fed three times a day.

Over the years, I have had a deep sense of anger, sadness and helplessness. Acting out on these emotions has led me to live a life behind bars since the age of eighteen. I have served four county years and a total of eleven years in state prison. I am thirty-four years old.

▣

SHADRACH PHILLIPS

Life Story

I was told I was born at St. Mary's Hospital,
here in San Francisco, in August,
the twenty-eighth, to be exact, in the year 1972.
My parents moved up north to Humboldt County.
Right above the Avenue of the Giants. In a house nestled
    between redwoods.
We did this move when I was two.
At or around this same time my li'l sister Mesha was born in
    Garberville near where we lived.
Parents grew marijuana.
Kept a lot of automatic gunz.

Parents grew marijuana. / Kept a lot of automatic gunz. / Learned to shoot them.

Learned to shoot them.

Learned police were enemies when they took Dad away for petty
tickets.

Divorces, custody battles, misc. kids, half brothers, sisters, step,
etc.

Too many to keep track of.

Child rapes, molestation, church madness, beatings, more
custody battles.

Moms kidnaps us, takes me and Mesha to New York
when I was eight.

Assume fake names.

Moms arrested by FBI.

Moms does time while courts put us back in house, molesting us.

Run away, so-called outta control.

Just tired of the molesters and slave drivers calling themselves
family.

Juvenile hall, ranch camp, youth authority, rehab, prison, prison,
prison, prison, prison.

For being homeless, trying to forget.

Tired of this subject, better left alone.

JASMINE BRYANT

Life Story

Hi. My name is Jasmine Bryant. I'm twenty-two years old. I'm
from a small city called Pittsburg/Antioch, California. I grew up
there from birth. I had a wonderful life until the age of fourteen
when my mother was murdered and my father was sent to prison
(not for the murder). I have five other siblings not including myself.
One sister and a brother. Three of them are biracial. I graduated
from Pittsburg High School in 2000. I have no children. I have
basically enjoyed my life. And, well, I still am. I have no regrets

about what has happened and hopefully what I'm going through right now at the moment shall pass as well. I love children and old people, and wish to work with them in the future. If nothing else works out in my life, I wish to help others so that maybe they'll stay on the right track and give back as well. You know change the "game" or just make "plain ole change." I was supposed to start college in July. The eighteenth to be on the up and up, and the way things are looking now, I might have to start next semester, which is in January. But hey, that's cool, just a minor set back. Well, I could write forever, but my fifteen minutes of fame is up. Thanks for listening.

Thanks for listening.

回

R. L. LOVE

I Didn't

My twelfth-grade graduation
A fine grand situation
My mother and father proud
My friends would cheer so loud . . . I didn't

That summer I worked at night
To help decide my plight
So gangs would leave me alone
I took the long way home . . . I didn't

My girl and I would go
To see the picture show
We hug and always kiss
She'd be the one I miss . . . I didn't

We plan for college true
We share the strongest view

But the Marines would be much better
The day I got that letter . . . I didn't

Of course I never said
The question no one read
Can I bet that kid
And yet I didn't . . . I never did.

🔲

WESLEY SIMMS

Nameless Name

Sadness is what I see in my reflection
I look dirty, used, and empty-eyed
Scars is what I'm made of, yet no one sees them
They're unhealable yet traceable, yet scars for a lifetime

My intimate moments is my essential reasoning to live
I cannot utter a feeling to communicate to be hated
But left unsaid is without her, so I continue to move
Sparkling flames of pain, fear of this one woman
No, not my bedroom lover, but the one who conceived me

In school I learned to laugh. It's my safe haven.
At home I pretend I'm invisible. I learn to hide.

Last night I felt her imprint across my face
The fingernails piercing my flesh as I bleed
Welts of pain from beatings as I lay or sit
The words echo of hate as I'm whipped unconscious

So a brick building becomes my loneliness
My friends' names are Pain, Fear, Terror, my only friends

Scars is what I'm made of, yet no one sees them

fear of this one woman / No, not my bedroom lover, but the one who conceived me

No one can see as I cry myself to sleep each night
My soul dwells with loneliness, yet my heart yearns for change

Totally sheltered, stripped of all pride
Pretentious courage, when it's fear I hide
Lonely and empty, and afraid of the unknown
Unloved as a child and teenager, and even full grown

No one to trust, no one to turn to
No family, no job skills, what am I to do?
Simply put, I'm scared, scared as I'll ever be
I can make it in jail, but can't seem to make it free.

WESLEY SIMMS

My Life, My World

Oakland, California is where I was born and raised. It's where you'll find broken families, shattered dreams, poverty, despair, and ghetto life.

I'm one of four kids. Each of my brothers and my sister have different fathers, Kenneth Willis, Karen Wilson, Marlon Maderios, and me—Wesley Simms. I can probably remember back to the ripe age of four or five where we stayed in the projects on Twenty-sixth Avenue, a little three-bedroom, one bathroom, kitchen and living room with a patio. My mother, who was twenty-eight or twenty-nine, was single at this time and had a job and made sure we had food and clothes. At any given night my father or one of my siblings' fathers would come spend a night. People would call my mother names like *whore* and *wino*.

I at five thought my mom was the most beautiful woman in the world. On my sixth birthday our life went from content to chaos. My father, who in my six years I may have seen twenty to

On my sixth birthday our life went from content to chaos.

thirty times, came back. The atmosphere changed immediately. My father, a true alcoholic, for some reason didn't like my two brothers and one sister, and in turn my brothers and sister stopped liking me. Understand that at six years old, my eight- and twelve-year-old brothers and my ten-year-old sister no longer talked with me or played with me. My father and mother began to drink heavily and stay out all night long. My father started beating my brothers and sister daily, my father would also slap, kick, or punch my mother, she'd have to wear sunglasses to hide her black eyes at work.

My mother started taking her misery out on the bottle and me. Like if my father was asleep or not at home, she'd find a reason to hit me or throw something at me. Our once clean house began to look junky and tacky. It was around this time I even saw a roach in our home. Life was for me becoming unbearable. Imagine my brothers and sister scared to be around my father, imagine they don't even like me, they hate me, my mom hates me, and my father hates them.

My only escape was staying outside. My friends lived in Apt. 3 and Apt. 6. Dwayne and Sherman stayed in Apt. 3. They had six sisters, their father was dead, and Helen, their mother, smoked pot all day. Their house was like a junkyard, roaches by the hundreds and mice in the cabinets, closets, under the beds, the house was filthy. I'd go and sit at the table every now and then, but usually I'd walk outside. My other friend in Apt. 6 was named Brian, he had a brother named Kim and a sister named Wanda. I had a crush on Wanda but she was four years older than me. Me, Brian and Dwayne was all seven and Sherman was eight but we was real close. They became my make-believe brothers.

One night around the year '71 my father left my mother and moved to Los Angeles. The family atmosphere returned somewhat, except my mother continued to drink and hate me. I can remember her beating my ass with an extension cord and yelling, "Every time I look at you, I see his no-good ass," talking about my pops.

My life became a living hell. Let's say my brother drank a juice out of the refrigerator, they would all blame it on me and my mom would whip me four to five times a week and tell me she hates me and I'll never be shit but a failure just like my daddy. I began staying out later and later.

I was the last one to know my father was dead. At eight years old I felt so lost, no one in my family cried, when I look back now everyone seemed happy. I ran away four days later. That was January 1973. Eight years and four months old, I ran away to a friend's house around the corner, stayed about five days, and his mom called some foster home people. I stayed in a foster home for eighteen and a half months in San Leandro with a loving family.

My auntie, my mom's oldest sister, fought to get me back. Reluctantly I went back home. At ten going on eleven, I quit school. My mom had moved and had a friend name Pat. Pat was around thirty-one or thirty-two, she was real nice and down-to-earth. Pat was staying with us. Her and my mom worked for New Bridge Foundation. I openly hated my mother and she openly hated me, but Pat would talk to me. She got me to go back to school, she used to give me money, fifty and sixty dollars, take me to the movies, shopping.

The first time we went swimming things changed. I remember her asking me how old I was. I was twelve, about two months from becoming thirteen. She said she wanted me to help her move into her apartment next Saturday. I say things changed because she'd do things like come in my room while I was in bed or come in the bathroom while I was in the bath or when I came in the house she'd hug me like a woman would hug a man, not like a woman would hug a child. She would call me downstairs, 'cause she slept on the couch, and when I got there she'd ask me to get something out the refrigerator or something then she'd say come here give Auntie Pat a big hug.

I'd never had a kiss or wasn't even into girls, so it wasn't an issue—I just felt happy to receive love from Auntie Pat.

Two nights before Saturday, she took me to a drive-in movie. I can't remember the name of the movie but it had a very sexual graphic scene in it. I'll admit I was impressed, excited and embar-

At that moment I felt so loved by Auntie Pat when she hugged me, she kissed me on my lips.

rassed at the same time. Pat started asking me all these crazy-ass questions like, Do you do your girlfriend like that? "No." Have you ever kissed a girl? "No." Come on, I bet all the girls want you. "No." Then she slid over, grabbed my hand, and was like, Stop being shy, now do you like that? I'm like, I don't know, I never tried it. She started smiling, she bet I'd be good and would probably have girls wanting more.

At the tender age of twelve my curiosity went from candy, tag, king of the mountain, sports, and hot wheels to women and sex. I remember the next day at school, how I'd look at those little girls differently. Friday night Auntie Pat snuck into my room and gave me a hardcore sex magazine and told me to keep it a secret. At that moment I felt so loved by Auntie Pat when she hugged me, she kissed me on my lips. I remember locking my bedroom door, turning on my room lamp and looking at that book title: *White Women Who Crave Big Black Men.* I remember dreaming of a girl that night, oddly enough the girl in my dream was black, nothing sexual, just a dream with her in it.

Saturday morning I was up to music and loud voices downstairs. When I made it downstairs it was my mom and Pat playing dominoes and Al Green on the record player. My mom actually kissed me and told me to get some breakfast.

This Saturday morning my mom cooked scrambled eggs, sausages, grits, and pancakes. While I'm fixing my plate, Pat walks in the kitchen and just stands there—but what she had on was crazy, a pair of shorts so tight I could see everything and a T-shirt with no bra. She could tell I was shy and embarrassed, but she was like, give me a hug. To be respectful I'm not going to go into all the details of me and Pat. Let's just say I got a full scholarship on sex education. By the time I was thirteen years old, I was getting paid by Pat and two of her friends. My mom never cared, though I believe she knew.

Stories from My Life

I. I was born in a small town in the state of Indiana called Fort Wayne. I come from a very large family of six brothers and two sisters. My mother was a single parent. She also never showed much physical affection. I can remember at a very early age watching Batman on TV and wanting that Batman suit. So I asked Mama. Her reply was, I'll see, baby. Days went by and weeks without that suit I wanted, so one day I took off to that store and walked right in and walked out and no one said anything. The lies came so easy from there on.

The lies came so easy from there on.

II. We had to share each others' shoes, they were passed down from one brother to the next. So we always encouraged each other to not wear down the shoes or clothing for fear of being worn out before these possessions became ours. Our Mama couldn't afford to shop at Sears or name-brand department stores. We went treasure hunting in secondhand stores and we would find all kinds of goodies. This was family time spent well, quality time. Of course we'd return home to the neighborhood to stop by the market to purchase dinner. Mama always asked us what we liked. Chicken was golden, next to fish. People would always stop by in those days and offer some of their catch of the day or from their deep freezer. But in our household, chicken ruled. Mama could make the best finger-lickin' chicken in the whole world.

The house would be filled with smells of sweetwater cornbread, yams, cake, and pie. Sometimes Mama would even let me help her prepare cakes. Son, she would say, here's the cake mix from the bowl. I loved the smell of the lemon flavoring. I remember asking this lady, Why does everyone come to our house from all over the neighborhood? Her reply was, Your mother allows people to be themselves. So I also remember my mother always treating drunks, homeless people all the same, letting them wash our car window, put groceries in the car after shopping. She would give them a few dollars and say something like, Baby, make sure you get something to eat, you hear? Yes, when I look back on my life growing up, I remember saying, I can't wait to leave this house when my brother or sister would hog the restroom or my mother wouldn't allow me to go to Playland at the beach. Those were the best times of my life growing up with a house full of sisters and brothers. Oh, how I miss those times.

III. Growing up I saw my brothers fighting and having fun playing games with girls. They always kept me locked out. I was loved, being the youngest boy. At some point my mother sat me down and explained that my brothers and sisters were moving to my aunt's and I would be sent for later. So I spent time living with my father's parents, the only child for a summer or two, I don't know for sure. But one day my brother Doug showed up at my grandmother's house and told me he came to bring me to where the rest of the family was, and we boarded this big bus and I realized now we were headed to California. Once we arrived things here were so different, faster than Fort Wayne. I was happy to be back with my family and the center of attention.

My favorite was banana pudding and sweet-potato pie.

School was good. I always had to follow my brothers' reputation of fighting, sports, basketball. I can remember our house was always the place to be during holidays or summer barbeques. My mother would prepare large meals and the table would be filled with all sorts of delights. My favorite was banana pudding and sweet-potato pie.

BROTHER LARRY MCCALLUM

Life Story

I grew up in the city of White Springs, Florida, which had a city pool, a big river called the Suwannee River in a colored black neighborhood, and an all-black school named Carver High School.

I was forced to go to school because my daddy's people were and still are very educated people. My daddy's name is Jake McCallum and my momma's name is Versie Lau Dye McCallum.

I was born in a house and delivered by a midwife or midnurse. I've heard a lot of things but who really knows, nobody but my momma and I have never asked her who delivered me.

April 7, 1955, I was born.

No brothers were with me when I grew up. Me and my oldest brother are five years apart in birth and age. My sister Linda Faye was born after me and Judy after her and my brother Wayne and my other brother Melvin. We are the first five born and the ones that I grew up with, closer than the other five children from my parents' union.

At the age of six I do remember getting to be bigger, growing and at the peak of beginning to learn a few things.

My daddy always used to take me with him on trips doing hunting, shooting dice, playing cards, and carrying the lamp to watch the older guys shoot dice, gamble for money, and learning how to shoot pool at the Dew Drop Inn run by Mr. Grech Brown.

As I continued to grow and go to school I was always getting into fights with other kids. They used to take your food during lunchtime, so if you didn't fight you didn't eat.

We used to go to the other end of the streets, to a place called Miss Kats and the Psychedelic Shack, another bar where me and my brothers and sisters went on over to party, dance, have fun as teenagers.

I'm in the eighth grade and now the government has integrated the schools.

Ninth grade on up to the twelfth grade must go to the integrated schools, different races of people.

I got along with the other kids of different color. The most violence was fights with the other city teenagers who always go for the macho behavior.

if you didn't fight you didn't eat.

Me and another student, a good friend of mine, used to play basketball all the time during school hours, physical education periods, also after school, and we partied a lot, going out with older women, trying to smoke cigarettes, especially when they was sixty-five cents a pack.

I got a job at the hospital and used to see the effect of long-term smoking of tobacco and that stopped me from ever wanting to smoke a cigarette.

Anyway, I graduated from another school thirty miles away, Columbia High in Lake City, Florida.

After I got suspended from my job I went into the army, volunteered for two years. I got a medical discharge, honorable conditions, not doing all my time in the army.

Next I got a new girlfriend, she got pregnant.

My life goes on and now I am traveling again.

In 1975 a boy was born, Freddie Phillips, he's got his mother's last name because she was not my common-law wife, just an outside woman friend of mine who had a baby from me. My life goes on and now I am traveling again.

Wandering from state to state I run into another lady who's got a boy from me, 1989. His name's Michael Alexander, on September twelfth, born in Phoenix, Arizona, and now I'm here in San Francisco 2004, October 2004, three years now.

TIM RODRIGUES

Life Story

I was born at Kaiser on Geary Street in San Francisco, 1960. My younger years were in San Rafael across the Golden Gate Bridge. I'm a second-generation Californian, my father was born in 1925 in Oakland. My mother was born at Ross Hospital in Marin, 1936. They met at a psychology class at SF State in 1955. I have a brother who was born in 1955 and a sister who was born in 1958. We all grew up together. Growing up in Marin during the sixties was a trip. My parents were Unitarian and Sunday school for me was tie-dyeing T-shirts and making God's eyes. When I was five years old, Janis Joplin came to the church to play. But no power, so an unplugged set.

回

MARK YBARRA

Life Story

I'm a Chicano. Spanish, English, French, and Mexican blood run through my veins. I'm a proud person one should ascertain. I don't push, but when push comes to shove, I don't worry about putting on gloves. I don't fight to win, I fight to survive. I'm a proud person. I'm a Chicano. The man of the house, master of my domain. This is my breeding my father explained, fight for survival even if the other must die. There's no honor in losing your life, not a game. This all sounds good, it all sounds good, and it would be if I were my dad.

My father would be proud of me. I'm a Chicano, master of my domain. I'm hearing his words, I'm fighting his fight. Hold on a second, this doesn't seem right. They call me Psychclone and say I'm insane. Could it be my father's to blame? This role that I'm playing is not really me.

I'm worried my father might learn, I talked my way out of a fight, I'm too young to kill and the thing is, I just might. My father left me when I was just twelve.

I'm sensitive and I love to laugh, and if you tell me a sad story I'll cry, imagine that.

I'm a Chicano, I'm a proud man.

I found comfort and I give it a name, I call it father, but not like the one who's insane.

My father left me when I was just twelve.

OLLIS FLAKES

If I Tried to Be Me

If I tried to be me
I just might succeed to gain the
Knowledge in growth
Empowering the mind
Providing all the information I need

If I tried to be me
I just might find
That what hinders my talents
Is all in the mind

And if I tried to be me
I'll begin to see
What type of strengths I possess
When clearly expressing me

But how will I feel
If I tried to be me?
With all this hatred and destruction
That the world can see

'N' if I tried to be me
I would try it right now
But I'm gonna need some help
Because I don't think I know how

*But how will I feel /
If I tried to be me?*

STEPHEN LOGAN

Liftoff

The USS Logan takes off again.
Houston, we have liftoff!

For so long I wonder why everything went wrong
You ask about my pain that drives me insane
I'll start with the tears that fell like rain
When my mother left me as a child
I ran wild with my fears and hidden tears
For my father I never got to meet
I heard stories of his street-life glories
My anger grew,
'Cause nobody knew the nightmare I lived through

A broken home, so unknown
My mother had a problem of drinking and using dope
But I learned to cope
With our secrets like how we lived
    and the people who surrounded us.
Bikers, criminals, tweakers, and the losers of the world
    were all in my home
So into the streets I'd roam

At school I had endless problems
Everyone thought I was a fool and so uncool
My *B*s looked like *D*s, dyslexia they said
I hated math I hated reading I hated it all
    I was so damn mad
I rebelled I fought my peers
These were the beginnings of my tears

In sixth grade I found my crowd
The stoners, the loners that had it all figured out

My mother had a problem of drinking and using dope

We were gonna smoke weed and run amok
    until they kicked us out
Or allowed me to just drop out

By ninth grade I was a full-grown blown criminal
Stealing cars smoking dope
Running away from home in and out of juvenile hall
Life was fast and hard
All too soon
I found my doom
In a spoon

I tried to find love in too many places
    in too many faces
That left me in empty and hollow places
Now I have needle-mark traces on my veins
From looking for love in one too many places

My heart has been hardened and sorrowed
From losing my friends to death,
    self-destruction, and the pen
Now I'm left all alone which has always been
    my biggest fear
And the cause of so many tears
Over too many lonely years

May Day, May Day. Houston,
    we have a problem
Yes, my life is a wreck and I've been lost
In a world of drugs and crime for so long
It's hard to remember any other way

GREG CARTER

Truth Decay

I was taught young to lie
Up until then, truth was as implicit as laughter.

When I look to the death of truth
it takes me back to about 1967. I was in the second grade
and I had done something grievously wrong,
or you would have thought so the way things turned out
that cold rainy day a long time ago.

When I was young I could not wait to get out of the house
and off to school. I saw fun in whatever I did,
until one day I thought it would be fun to sneak
    into the cloakroom
and reach into Richard Plunkett's lunchbox
and remove his Hostess fruit pie, cuz, Mom
    —god bless the country girl
that she was—her idea of a snack
    to augment a lunch was a banana.

I don't know how many times I saw him pull out
    some Ho-Hos or Snowballs and say,
    "Lookie what I got."
It wasn't the sun that peeked through that day
    to shine precisely down
on that wrapper as he lifted it out of the box,
    it was the snide look on his precocious
face that doomed his callous dessert.

Later that day events were taking place that were
    going to change the way I did things for a long, long time.

12:15 PM and the pie is missing, the investigation has begun.
I got a sinking feeling in my stomach that isn't getting any
    better, I got a note pinned to my shirt
    and I am going to deny this until my dying day.
It was right about that time that we heard that old George
    Washington cherry tree crap about how if you tell the truth
    you will not get in trouble.
I guess I lasted about a week. It was a rainy day
and my father graciously offered to give me a ride to school.
I remember looking over at him and for the life of me I cannot
    believe the words that came out of my mouth,
    "Father, I ate the pie."
As he hit the brakes he backhanded me at the same time and I
    remember bouncing off the back window. And I knew right
    then that the truth would serve no more purpose in my life
    and I ran with that, to tell you the truth,
    no pun intended, right up until now.

It should not be this way because as far as I'm concerned
    truth is the death of wrong been done and
    where will we go from here.

MARK HALL

Issues

I believe that we are who we are, I am who I am, because of the "issues" surrounding my life. The issues directly influenced the choices I made. So about the issues . . .

    When my father (who was never Daddy) left Momma when she was the ripe old age of nineteen and I was just two, and when he'd call from time to time to write when you was six or seven to say he'd be there to take you to the park or to the zoo or for a ride in his car but never seemed to find his way to where you are, well . . . that's the beginning of an issue.

So Momma marries this man when you're ten who has kids of his own and all you really want is to "fit in" and be one just like the rest, and you really do try your ten-year-old best . . . but somehow it never ever seems to work out that way . . . and you're always reminded that you're different . . . well that's an issue too . . . and it grows and you grow and your real Daddy still never shows and yeah, you guessed it, these issues grow and grow . . . and grow.

And you never seem to "fit in" and that's all you ever really wanted to do.

So maybe to fit in I'll do what everybody else do. Yeah, I'll smoke weed and cut class and then maybe you'll let me fit in with you.

But I never quite fit in and that's issue two, or is it three? Maybe it's an extension of issue number one, passed on from father to me. Man, who knows? Who cares? Bury it, hide it, never let 'em see you sweat . . . buy cars, get jobs, pretend like you're the shit, when in reality you're a piece of the puzzle that never really does fit.

Bury it, hide it, never let 'em see you sweat

On and on you go and along comes a girl. Not just any girl, it's you and me, baby, me and you against the world. And all is cool for a while, until life throws you its next curve. It's a big disease with a little name and your life will never be the same. So yo' baby, she dies, and even though you're lucky enough not to be infected, you are affected in a hell of a way. Yo' baby's gone and here comes the rain, and fuck it, I'm about to smoke this coke 'cause I ain't ready for this kind of pain. So that's what I do in an effort to hide from all these issues that I have inside.

Yeah, I been clean now for a minute and I've learned that it is the issues that give me permission to do the things I did. Those issues I ran from but could never hide. So if you ever want to know what makes people do what they do, just look at the issues. They're what make me, me and make you, you.

When I was born, my dad was so happy that he started drinking early that day and never stopped.

WILFREDO AGUILAR

Life Story

I was born in Central America in a country named El Salvador in 1962, December 26 at around 10:00 AM in a general hospital. When I was born, my dad was so happy that he started drinking early that day and never stopped. He was supposed to register my birth at the Hall of Justice but he forgot and two days later, he remembered and went in December 28, 1962, so my birth certificate says December 28, 1962, even though my real birthday is December 26. I knew my dad was an alcoholic since the day he met my mom.

I was a troubled child. My life in a poor country was hard, especially when you lived on a block where around the corner was three blocks of canteens, bars of prostitutes, and a lot of violence. I remember one time I witnessed one fight in which the two were fighting with machetes, and one of them swung so fast that it decapitated the other one. I saw the head falling down on the floor and rolling down towards the chairs and tables.

While on the bus going my way to the U.S.A., the "Land of Opportunity," for better education, I did not know what was waiting for me up there. Looking from inside the window of the bus, I saw the green land and trees, the faraway mountains, and on occasion a river or a bridge. At some moments I felt so lonely and far away from home that I got homesick. My heart felt like I was leaving something very precious, that my life was being left behind or like my life had just stopped.

I had always believed that all struggles were because I felt I was an inferior person who maybe did not deserve anything good. At first I thought that I had brought too much pain to all people around me. Maybe I brought bad luck to all who got too close to me, that I created a big barrier, a defense attitude, a wall of pain and suffering. This came along with my shyness and self-pity, also inferiority.

This made a sadness that triggered madness and violence towards anyone that I crossed. Deep inside this feeling.

回

BRIAN BAIRD

Life Story

I grew up in Dallas, Texas, in an upper-middle-class family who raised me fairly well, I suppose. I had all the necessities a child could ever want in life. Private school gave me a good education, piano lessons taught me about culture, cotillion taught me manners and social graces, sports taught me to be a team player, my sister taught me about sharing, and of course my father taught me the value of money, while my mom was my best friend. I went to block parties and summer camp, sometimes in New Mexico, sometimes in Cape Cod. The one thing I never learned was how to appreciate these things and to be happy.

I was always good at everything I did. I have a 142 IQ so I did well in school, won state recitals in piano, including being invited twice to participate in the Von Cliburn Competition, which is the World Series or Superbowl of piano competition. I ran on the cross-country team, soccer team, and junior varsity basketball teams. In the seventh grade I was offered a full math scholarship to Duke University. Somewhere along the line, I also succeeded in being addicted to drugs and alcohol.

By the 10th grade, I dropped out of high school, stopped playing piano, and left home. Little did I know that a lifetime of bad decisions had begun.

The first time I did drugs I had just started at a new school. I was eleven years old. I was spending the night at a new friend's house and we were smoking cigarettes. He pulled out a pipe with marijuana in it and said, Here, try this. I took a hit and blew it out. (I didn't inhale, mind you, so I said, Hey, that's cool.) He told me

The one thing I never learned was how to appreciate these things and to be happy.

*Most of my life
has been spent
searching for the
perfect feeling, the
goodness that I
never believed I
had in me.*

to hit it again, inhaling this time. I did and started coughing like crazy. I hated it. After a few minutes, my mind changed, though, as the weed took its effect on me. As we smoked some more, drank a little, and listened to Led Zepplin, I realized that this was better than I'd ever felt before. New kid at school, immediately accepted by people, it was awesome. This was something I had to keep doing. Little did I know where it would eventually take me.

Over the years since then I have wasted much potential and made many bad decisions in my quest for happiness. I've been to twelve rehabs, spent two years preaching and witnessing to other drug addicts and prostitutes while a member of Victory Outreach Church. I've been married and divorced twice and I have a nine-year-old daughter, who currently lives with my parents in Dallas because I have been too busy getting high to be a good father. Or maybe I am a good father, since I have made sure she is provided for and in the best place.

Most of my life has been spent searching for the perfect feeling, the goodness that I never believed I had in me. When success and being good at things got boring, I went on to more challenging things. Getting away with doing wrong was it. I never, ever felt challenged in my life, be it through music, church, school, or whatever. Playing cat and mouse with the cops has been my biggest challenge, which to an extent has been fun, because my brain gets stimulated trying to come up with new ways to beat the system. Identity theft, which is what I am in jail for, allows me to do everything that I did wrong in my life differently. It's like a second chance.

While I may have thrown away opportunities in my life, I've only failed at one thing. Beating the system. I always get caught eventually, because no matter how much I come up with by hustling, it's never enough. So I get out of jail and try it again, doing a few things differently.

BRIAN BAIRD

Why Am I Afraid to Be Me?

Why am I afraid to be me?
Is it because I'm hurt and lonely?
Don't I have some good qualities?
Wasn't I raised by a good family?

The things I have learned from society
Tell me to do things traditionally
Do well in school. Get As and Bs
Go on to a prestigious university

Hold on for a second. Step back and see
What happens when I'm not allowed to be me
I start being rebellious
Doing things on the sly
Leaves people wondering, "Why? Oh why?"

You're so very bright and talented too
My God! Your IQ is 142!

The things I enjoy to this very day
Are writing, computers, and making soufflés
Yes, I thoroughly love to cook
But pick up a book? Okay, look!

I don't mind making the grades
But only if I can do it my way
My teacher says, "Do this, this way," you see
Another way comes from my family
Throw in a tutor or two for good luck
Now I feel like a sitting duck

**Only the Dead
Can Kill**

*Why do you think I
steal identities?*

You see, my whole life I've been taught how to live
I've learned how to take, and I've learned how to give
But there is one thing that makes me want to flee
That is someone telling me how to be me

Hell, I don't know how to be me,
Why do you think I steal identities?
I also steal checks and some credit cards
At least I haven't yet stolen your car

I'm constantly trying to be someone else
Putting my own life up on a shelf
Collecting dust, there I will be
Until I figure out my own identity

I'm getting too old for this shit, I think
I should have listened to one of my shrinks
And stayed in school and played it cool
Maybe instead of jail, I'd be out by the pool

That sounds like fun, I'm sure you'll agree
I'm glad I'm finally learning about me
Slowly but surely gaining my identity

Today I'm not afraid to be me
Regardless of what other people may see
I know who I am today, I, myself, and me

Life Story

I come from a family of four children. I am the second to the eldest of these children. There are three boys and one girl, my sister being the youngest of us all. Both my mother and father are, to this day, still married. This, of course, is based on information from two years ago now. I am currently on a boycott. Growing up as a kid was not the easiest for me.

I suppose I was about ten years old. Whenever my parents went out I would rummage through their stuff looking for their stash. One day I came across their weed. I am thinking, I bet this stuff is great. I proceeded to take a great number of them, not thinking they had them counted out one by one. Needless to say, when I got caught I claimed I knew nothing of where their weed was. Thinking if I held out long enough I would get to keep the weed. Wrong. I was made to stand in the corner. After hours and well into the night I stood my ground of my innocence. I knew nothing. I finally gave in. I just couldn't take it standing in the corner. And besides, my nose was getting sore. My mother was crying. I asked my mother what is the matter. She said, He left. I said, Who? She said, Your father has left. He even took all the money we had hid away for that rainy day. Mom, what's a rainy day? That's a day when you need a little extra money for those unexpected problems in life. I said, Oh, where did he go? She said, I only wish I knew. I told her, That's okay, Mom, I'll get a job to help you out.

I was forced out of the home at the age of fourteen. This was due to seven years of stealing their weed. My mother had enough of me stealing their weed so she told my father in front of me, "Either he leaves (me) or I leave (my mother)." My father had to make a hard choice. It was me he chose to throw out of his and their life.

That is when I started the roller coaster of foster homes. The issue that kept coming up was that my parents refused to pay the price it cost to keep me in foster care. It got to a point where I did finally end up in a group home. I ended up attending seven different

While away in the group home, my biological family moved away out of state and didn't even tell me they moved.

high schools. While away in the group home, my biological family moved away out of state and didn't even tell me they moved.

One of my placements in foster care was a home where it was a requirement to do hard labor in order to be fed any meals. If you did not work, you were not fed. Yet another home I was placed in was where the foster parents, from my point of view, were in it for just the money. The mother had it down to a science. She even had our meals portioned out to the exact amount of what was recommended as the minimum for each child to eat, thanks to her trusty old scale she used every time.

Pops, on the other hand, was just as scary. Imagine a person who sat around and ate cigarettes (smokes) straight from the pack. Man, have you ever chewed on a cigarette? He did this for health reasons. He was told by his doctor he could no longer smoke ever in his life again. Plus us kids were told he enjoyed this new form of consumption, plus it was loaded with good old vitamin C.

As a child, I just knew I would be like every kid on the block. I would have a nice car, go to the prom, then off to college. Well, I still have yet to get my license.

DAVID GREEN

My Life in One Sentence

I was born in 1963 in a small town in New England, raised by hillbilly good ole boys who drank beer and jacked deer by the light of the moon, raised from this I couldn't wait to get away from the dirt roads and pickup trucks and find the bright lights and big city, having found that at the age of thirteen I got busy, quickly ruining my health and any chance I had for a "normal" life, not that I'm complaining about the life I've led, I've had great sorrow, should have been dead years ago but I guess God has decided I haven't paid my debt yet, I've tasted recovery and spent a few years clean, lost track of time and wound up back on the treadmill, back and forth to the pen, in the county for a minute, on the street for a minute less, I'm hoping for a last chance to get on my horse and ride on into the sunset with my saddlebags full of riches.

DAVID GREEN

My Real Life Story (or At Least My Version of It)

I think my life really began for me at the age of three when I died. I was riding my tricycle on a second-story balcony when I went through the railing and landed on my head, crushing it. I died on the way to the hospital. I was in a coma for six months. When I was released from the hospital I was not allowed to cry because I could have had blood clots break loose in my head. I was the youngest of four kids and when my brothers made me cry, they got punished for it. What power I had! Of course my brothers hated me. Who wouldn't.

I first experienced acceptance from my brothers around the age of six when they started having sex with me. At last I had found my place in the family. The versatile boy-toy who could entertain the whole neighborhood with his feats of agility. So of course I perfected the art of acceptance quickly and thoroughly.

I first experienced acceptance from my brothers around the age of six when they started having sex with me.

Everything was going along just fine until we all hit puberty and my brothers became interested in girls. I personally had no problems doing what I did as it was really the only time I felt wanted in my life. I was now thirteen and beginning to form a sense of independence. I rebelled and for the first time in my life stood up for mine.

This was real hard for my family to deal with. My mother put me in the youth authority in Maine, locked me up with thousands of guys who had nothing to do but work out, they removed all the women and called that punishment. Imagine that.

Let's be real, I'm not afraid to be locked up with a bunch of men. I'm afraid I'm gonna die locked up and I'm gonna miss something I deserve.

TINA TATE

Life Story

I keep doing what I'm doing 'cause I am used to the fast money. I really am tired of this stuff tho'.

My name is Tina Marie Tate. I was born in Richmond, California on May 24, 1983. My mother is Carol Hollis and my father is Lucillus Anthony Tate. I have one brother and four sisters. I went to elementary school in Richmond. I started junior high in Richmond and finished junior high in Sacramento where my father moved when I was twelve years old. I then moved back to Richmond with my mom and started high school in Richmond on home studies. I started working for a while at a day care. Then I started out my criminal activity in San Francisco. I've been arrested several times for selling drugs. I did five months out of my life in San Francisco County Jail. I keep doing what I'm doing 'cause I am used to the fast money. I really am tired of this stuff tho'. I have a li'l sister that I take care of. So I really need to stop, so I can be there for her. I'm not going to say I'm going to quit committing crimes for life, but I am going to slow down because I'm going too fast. All I can do is pray and ask God for help.

JOHN TONINI

My Life Story in Twenty Minutes

I am an only child of middle-class parents who have poured into me all the love as well as all their desires for success. They sent me to all the right schools, sacrificed to give me anything I asked for, and in return I was expected to excel in everything, academics, sports . . . to be a perfect child who should grow up into a perfect adult.

Unfortunately for me I lived up to my end of this unspoken, unsigned agreement and bought into my parents' goals and made them my own for many years. Teachers, friends, society, books, movies, and commercials conspired to reinforce these values. Go to college, get a great job, make money, drive a nice car, wear nice clothes. Of course I should want these things and of course they would bring me happiness.

So I went to college and worked my ass off. Graduation, one goal achieved, but I was no happier. Landed some good jobs, lots of pressure, long workdays but not too much happiness. Started making money.

Was I happy? No. I just wanted more money.

Was I happy? No. I just wanted more money.

🔲

LATASHA SMITH

Life Story

My name is Latasha Smith. I'm thirty-seven years old, born in Houston, Texas. I am the youngest of fifteen children. I have four children: two boys, two girls. My oldest is twenty, my youngest son is sixteen, my oldest girl is eighteen, my youngest is fourteen. They are living in Houston with my aunt and family.

I started snorting coke at an early age, as well as selling drugs. I've had clean time by the years and the months. I just relapsed May 1, 2005. I would have had two years clean next month on the eleventh. My relapse was due to the loss of my brother and one cousin.

🔲

MICHAEL FISHER

The Story of My Life

I lost my entire family because they didn't accept my choice to be gay.

My name is Michael Fisher and I am thirty-four years old. There really isn't much to tell. I lost my entire family because they didn't accept my choice to be gay. That was when I was sixteen. So I've pretty much learned to live my life alone or attempt to limit the people that I have around me. As a result, I suffer from manic depression. I have since I was seventeen. Everything that I feel, other than anger, I hold deep within. Anyway, I grew up in a mixed family and lived in a mixed neighborhood. My mother is black/Indian and my father is white. I've always had an open mind and I will always do whatever I can to hold on to that. I've never had to endure racism of any kind. Only homophobia, and that always comes from the black side of my race. So as I've said, I've stayed pretty much to myself. To be honest, I prefer being by myself rather than being around people sometimes. People always tend to judge me first by my appearance and sexuality before they even get to know me. So I don't even bother getting close to people. What's the sense. I prefer to deal with open-minded people who are your friend regardless of your sexuality or skin color or social class. My biggest passion in life is to become a fashion designer. I have always been interested in clothing. Specifically women's clothing, which is another reason why I choose not to be around people a lot. A lot of people don't understand how a man can design women's clothes. I don't care though, because someday I will accomplish my dream.

People look down on me when I tell them that I've sold myself for money. But I don't care, I survived

I've grown up knowing what it's like to be around people with money and being on the streets homeless, selling myself for money. People look down on me when I tell them that I've sold myself for money. But I don't care, I survived and have seen more things than the average person has. I am not ashamed of anything that I've gone through in my life. No one is perfect and no one has any room to judge me. My life has been an okay life. From eighteen to twenty-two I used to be a print male model in Missouri. To be honest I was happiest then. I wasn't making thousands of dollars an hour. But I did get a lot of work. Usually catalog work for Dillard's or Macy's and fashion shows for senior citizens or black-tie events and fund-raisers. I really had fun then and I wanted it to go further but certain things happened to stop that. I got a real thrill seeing myself in catalogs or newspaper ads. The money I was paid wasn't enough to buy a Mercedes, but all of my bills were paid.

SEAN REYNOLDS

Life Story

The year is 1980, my mother was forty-one, my father was forty, and I was thirteen. The afternoon is at a start, with a pleasant feel in the air. My dad and I were preparing for a trip to San Francisco; we were living in Redding, California, actually, though we were living thirty miles outside of it, up towards the foothills on a piece of property that had a thickness of trees and bushes throughout. Oh, the beauty the area held—the birds of many varieties, even bald eagles flew about—I believe a nest sat in one of the trees in the near distance. Mountain lions, bears, coyotes, and deer that roamed freely with no boundaries. But for this day, boundaries were being made by my father. Before we left, I kissed my mother good-bye, and we were off down a three-and-a-half-hour road to San Francisco.

The day was beginning to darken upon the arrival into San Francisco. My dad and I unpacked. Soon after he disappeared to call home. A half hour later he returned in a rage. He then insisted on packing for no reason—we were back home nearly four hours later.

The house was dark—no one was home. I figured out at this point the reason for returning home was because my mother wasn't home—my dad is a jealous type, after all. Shortly after our return,

The house was dark—no one was home.

my father quickly disappeared into the dining room to a cabinet that housed the guns—yes, guns—and yes, that's what he went in there to get. Moments later, I heard my mother's car moving up the long driveway—nearly a quarter of a mile long. Soon after, I snuck out the darkened quiet house, running across the dark lawn, and then stopping where my mother would park. My mother parks, stops the engine, and opens the door. I then tell her to stand still and stay quiet, and then my father opens the door—we hear his steps move atop the porch—silence—a click of a gun—silence—more silence—I then yell, If you shoot her, you'll be shooting me first. More silence—silence—and then a movement of steps from the porch and he disappears into the dark woods.

THANE POUNCY

Dark Me

I'm dark, that I can say, and I will always be that way, that is my makeup God has me wear. It is also a beauty that I can share, so deep in shade and in the most wonderful way, my look is something that no one else can chameleon.

I'm one in a million, you wonder why am I not sad, because I'm not the only one with this shade, you see, there are many, but . . .

There is only one dark me, some have even gotten mad at this fact, even have called me black, but that can't be me, because black is just a color, you see, with an end. But that ain't me, not if my mother is the same shade as me, and we ain't nowhere near the end, you see, because of my grandmother, rest her soul, she died at eighty-two years old. But before she was put here, there was my great-grandmother who was the same shade as me, and she died at ninety-three, and she gave my mother her name, Girtha Lee Lewis. Get my point, we go back quite some time, me and my shade.

So don't call me black.

My son will bring this same shade right back or maybe even my daughter's shade will. But one thing for sure, this dark me is for real, not something, or a phase, me and my dark self will be here for the rest of our days to come.

this dark me is for real, not something, or a phase

🔲

KIMBERLEY WRIGHT

Life Story

My name is Kimberly Wright, also my name is Sheila Jean Aton. I was born in Frankfurt, Germany, and adopted there. My birth mom was thirteen years old and was raped by a black military man. I was adopted by Mrs. and Mr. Wright. My mother was a native of San Francisco. I grew up here in San Francisco. I went to Junipero Serra child care. I went to Saint Michael's Middle School. And high school. I went to Abraham Lincoln High School. I was freshman-class secretary. My mom is now about to retire from the federal government. My grandmother was diagnosed with cancer but didn't tell the family until one week before she passed away for her reasons. I am playing sports in my high school sophomore years. Grandmother passed. Officially, before my grandmother passed, I graduated. I'm very proud to say I'm the first grandchild to graduate from high school. I get into drugs. I go into recovery. I get arrested. This has been my pattern and also the consequences of my behavior. I have two children, Malcolm, the oldest, and Martha, the youngest. My mom's adopted them. Because of my bad choices and my addiction, I lost my parental rights. I'm now in jail again for my behavior.

I was born in Frankfurt, Germany, and adopted there. My birth mom was thirteen years old and was raped by a black military man.

🔲

*when I'm allowed
to hit the air again
it seems like
everything changes*

JANICE ARMSTRONG

Rising out of the Dark

My name is Janice Marie Armstrong. I'm thirty-seven years of age. I was born in Martinez, California, and raised partially in Louisiana. I came back to California at the age of fifteen, resided in Richmond, California, for a while, then moved to San Francisco and here's where I've remained prior to moving all over California. I've been many places, some by force and some by choice.

I really don't know where to start because there is so much that has went on in my life, there is so much that I'm still being healed from, even from a li'l girl. It seems like life has taken me so fast or crept up on me every time I got out of one thing or get healed from something else. Same thing with relationships. I wonder where will it stop. I pray every night that it will stop here while I have a level head and my mind made up. It seems I've been doing that for the last year and a half. The reason I say that is because I have good intentions when I'm here in situations I can't get out of, but then when I'm allowed to hit the air again it seems like everything changes, my whole being changes, and it repeats itself all over again. That's why I say it's a miraculous thing because I wind up back in jail praying again. It may seem funny but it's really sad. No, not really. I really think it's a blessing. It gets harder and harder every time I don't do right. I pray I get it right this time.

During my first year in my drug addiction, I wanted to get high and I would go off and get high with guys I barely knew and they would want to have sex with me and I would refuse or just sit there and when everything was gone and I was ready to go, they would get violent with me, like bust my head open. I've had my arm broken, I've had my head busted wide open, I've been even left for dead, raped in one of the worst ways anyone could ever be raped in.

DWIGHT HAMMOND

Life Story

Dwight Lewis Hammond Jr. was born in Grand Rapids, Michigan, at the Butterworth Hospital in 1964. His mother was Mary Gilbert before she married his father, and she lived on Gilbert Street. Her parents were well-to-do and her brother was the chief of police, Russell Gilbert, who is still so, to my knowledge, but I haven't checked in a while. You know how things can change.

Dwight had a sister and her name was Renee although they never got to see each other growing up. Only on two occasions were they permitted to see one another. You see, their mother died when Dwight was about two years of age, to my disappointment as well. This story is only a one-sided tale about Dwight Lewis Hammond Jr., me.

My mother was killed in an automobile accident. I was told by my father that he would come home and find me in shitty diapers so I grew up trying to convince myself that it didn't matter she was gone. My father wasn't there either. He left me with her parents until he caught her mom. You see she had a lot of valuable things so she let me live locked up in the closet. Then my dad found out so he took me to East Lansing to my aunt Lena's place who was on the Indian council. But as you can guess with all those wild Indians drinking and getting high, there was no space for me. So once again I was moved on.

Finally a home. I moved in with my grandma and grandpa and aunt and uncle, my dad's ma and pa and brother Eddie and sister Sue. It was very nice there. My grandma was an Indian who loved God and me too. We canned food and made baked goods together and we had a deal. If I could catch it she would clean it so when other kids were at school, I'd be looking for a different school, a school of fish so we could eat, or a rabbit or a squirrel.

I was deemed uncontrollable at four years old. At five I almost died. A bloodhound thought I was a steak and split my head open

You know how things can change.

I was deemed uncontrollable at four years old.

I lived in a tree house and hunted and fished every day, which was good because the tourists would buy the salmon for five to ten dollars apiece and that was a lot of candy and Dairy Queen.

and I loved it anyway. They prescribed me speed, at that time Ritalin.

My uncle was a boxer. He would have me put the 16 oz gloves on and we would go at it every day, which led to trouble for me later down the road. My aunt was a concert pianist but everybody in the family played music. I grew up playing bluegrass and gospel mostly by ear. The first song I composed was the Little Eskimo who got stuck in the snow bank at the age of four. My grandfather was a kind man who worked with his hands. He was a carpenter who grew up in the Depression. He shoveled coal during that time but was a carpenter who worked in the garden a lot and built bird-houses for Grandma. She loved her bird colonies. We had every kind of bird that lived in Michigan except bluejays. I was given a wrist rocket slingshot and a BB-gun rifle to keep them away.

I miss them still, my grandparents. I was taken away from them at the age of eleven. Actually I ran away after my grandmother died of cancer. It was a very horrible painful experience watching her die. She died in our home. It was really hard on Grandpa, and the state said that he could no longer keep me.

I lived in a tree house and hunted and fished every day, which was good because the tourists would buy the salmon for five to ten dollars apiece and that was a lot of candy and Dairy Queen. Well, that lasted until my uncle caught me outside the Dairy Queen. I never knew he could move so fast. It was like a hawk catching a rabbit. He snatched me off that bike so quick it was like I wasn't even moving.

They sent me to a shelter home and then my dad showed up to save the day. You see, the state wanted to put me in training school but he took me with him to Middleville, where he lived with Mary Ann Gamble at the Copper Door Lounge, which was a hotel bar and restaurant. He was her boyfriend, I guess, but one thing was for sure, I didn't fit in and I definitely wasn't wanted there although I tried.

I remember still the silverware on the left, the silverware on the right, the fingerbowls, wearing a monkey suit, and the teacups, the poodles, Mary Ann's children, the Brass Anchor Yacht Club, the private colonies they owned on Cob Lake, the Pontoon Company, all the nice houses and cottages and yet they still found somebody from the paper and they boarded me out when she had had enough of me. I guess my dad was just using her for her money and so I was a good way to get out of putting out, but that didn't last long.

Staying with the lady in the paper, Miss Boardsman, how ironic her last name was the same as her occupation for cash. After I wrecked her kid's minibike she kicked me out so my dad boarded me out with Fern Harper. She was one of the cocktail waitresses who worked for them. They had a farm which I worked on each day. They had a big cornfield, horses, chickens, pigs, cows, and a lot of cats. There were two girls, Malena and Dorene, and two boys, Maurice and me. Maurice was gay and so was Dorene so I didn't think it strange when me and Malena decided to do a little hanky-panky. I think we were just trying to bring some natural order back to the place. But, nonetheless, it was back on the road again.

This time I moved in with my dad's brother Lime and his wife, Marlene, and two kids, Karen and Brian, the latter of the two has the same birthday as me, 4/27/64, not the same year though. That didn't last long. Lime didn't work and Marlene got laid off and then I went with my dad's sister Jinny and her husband and three kids, Mark, Bobby, and Linda.

Me and the boys were always going crazy. My aunt would whip me good. She was an alcoholic and I believe was hooked on speed or just had the worst case of nerves I ever saw. She couldn't even hold a cigarette without shaking. At any rate they would have people come over to play bridge, canasta, pinochle, and assorted card games for money and for recreation. They would go out bowling a lot.

My uncle Robert Detiaf was a phenomenal man. He would do all this and play with the kids in the park next door to his house and work as a foreman at Ken Dillard's plastic plant. He wasn't a normal foreman. He would work right alongside of his men until the job was done. He liked to hunt deer with a bow and arrow and make his own wine. Those were his hobbies. He died of muscular dystrophy. His daughter was born with crippled legs but she wore leg braces for years and fought against it and healed herself and became a cheerleader, then became a first-string basketball player. I really hold a great admiration for both of them. They will always be heroes to me.

Well, back to the drawing board. That lasted until one day Sonny and my dad's sister Judy and their kids came to visit us and they were drinking and Mark and Bobby had bats and were terrorizing me. Well, Bob had enough so he said, "All right, boys, come here. You want to fight Mark, little Lewie?" That's what they called me. Needless to say, years of boxing every day paid off that day. I beat every inch of his body black and blue. My aunt was throwing up when I went in after getting all the praise of the spectators. She didn't beat me bloody with the coffee pot cord until the next day and then I ran away. I took the bicycle and rode to where my aunt Judy and uncle Sonny lived. I was kind of tired once I arrived seeing how it was over fifty miles. My aunt gave me up but not to my aunt Jinny. I went to my aunt Sue and Ron. I had fun there. I played basketball and went mushroom picking and played music every day.

TIMOTHY SCOTT

Tim's Life Story: The Younger Years

I'm twenty-one years of age now. I was raised in San Francisco's Lakeview district. I had my sixth birthday in Lakeview. I lived with a big family, my mom, pops, brother, sister, cousins, and aunt (my dad's sister).

I went to Jose Ortega Elementary School. My pops was disabled, so he had SSI to help my mom pay the bills. My big sister and the younger of my oldest brothers and I had a paper route to help pay bills also. That was kind of fun though. I stopped doing the paper route when I was eleven years old, started when I was eight years old.

After the paper route, my brother and I started helping the elderly do things around their house. We got to keep that money. When I turned thirteen years old I quit working for other people and started hanging on the block. The block was full of dope dealers, gun slangers, and pimps. I started out just playing with some of the other young kids my age. Some of them I had went to school with so it was cool to do whatever we did. Things like steal drinks from out the corner store and smoke these cigarette-type things called bitties. I thought I was getting "high" so I kept smoking. It wasn't until I was at my best friend's house when I really felt what "high" felt like. His big brother sold weed and left it lying around sometimes. So my boy and I seen some and we looked at each other like, "Let's do it" (smoke the weed).

So by the time I was fourteen years old, I had been smoking and drinking my ass off. Yeah, I went to school but only cuz that's where the girls were. All my homies that went to my high school was doing just what we thought was the thing to do. Getting high. Never went to class, always came back for lunch to sell the weed, the bitties, and sometimes the drink. Then after school, if we didn't have money, we'd get on the bus on the way home and take people's pagers so we could sell them, take the money and buy weed. The more pagers, the more weed. Of course, we kept money for food but most of us would rather get weed than food.

My mom and dad broke up when I was fourteen and a half so that left me and my pops by ourselves, then I was on welfare, and Pops still had SSI. My brother was not around cuz he was caught up in the street life. My sister had moved out before Moms left and had kids of her own. I had to take care of my dad by myself. That put a lot on my shoulders.

My pops taught me how to drive at that age. I learned fast. I was driving everywhere at fourteen almost fifteen, or I think I was

I had to take care of my dad by myself. That put a lot on my shoulders.

twelve or thirteen. I was still in the eighth grade when I started driving. I have a screwed-up memory so bear with me. Anyway, I never had time anymore to myself. I was paying bills, writing checks, food shopping. I quit school a little after ninth grade.

▣

ANDRE MAXIMILIAN

Life Story

I became an addict because methamphetamine was introduced to me by others and was good for sex and dancing in the clubs, and losing body fat, etc.

I was born in Casablanca, Morocco. I was educated in France, I was at the university. The name is Université de la Picardie. I left for Paris to study at the Université de la Sorbonne, France. I decided to come to America to become a psychologist. I finished my senior year at San Francisco State University. I got my BA (in organizational psychology/clinical). I got accepted to USF to finish my Masters. I became a substitute teacher with the Unified School District. But I always had a job in the big hotels. I was a banquet manager at the Hilton Hotel, the Sheraton Palace, the Hyatt Regency, the Mark Hopkins. I became an addict to methamphetamine, and I started to come to jail.

I became an addict because methamphetamine was introduced to me by others and was good for sex and dancing in the clubs, and losing body fat, etc. Also it made me glamorous like the Hollywood style. Then of course when I do speed I meet other people, they do the same thing, and some of them you just want to be with and speed makes it easy to hang out together and have fun.

For the last six years of my addiction, from success to destruction, the price of my addiction is heavy. I lost my freedom, and I said, I have to stop using speed. Obviously I didn't stop. I am here in jail.

I don't want to talk about my family because I need to talk about myself first. Because I am still an addict. When I stop my addiction I will talk about my family.

MICHAEL ROTHSTEIN

Life Story

Hello to everyone! Thank you for this wonderful opportunity to introduce myself and to tell you my life story in the next twenty minutes, so that's roughly twenty-four seconds per year for all you mathematicians and rocket scientists out there who stumble upon my autobiography.

So are ya ready? Buckle up for safety 'cause here we go . . .

My name is Michael Alan Rothstein. I was born at Hameron Hospital on May 22, 1956, at approximately 6:00 PM (PST). Of course I don't remember what day of the week it was.

My mother's name is Nancy, maiden name of Herbst. She is German and English. My father's first name is Baron and I believe we've covered the last. My father is 100 percent Jewish.

Growing up primarily in my mother's and stepfather's home, since my mother and father divorced when I was five, I was the primary pawn in the religious tug-of-war between Catholicism and the Jewish/Hebrew teachings.

I essentially grew up in a very dysfunctional, abusive, alcoholic family of the sixties, until the age of seventeen when I enlisted in the U.S. Army. I was the object of much abuse, as I was a chronic bed wetter until the age of thirteen. My mother insisted that I wet the bed for attention; however, I had surgery when I was nearly thirteen for an enlarged bladder.

My mother was a very dominating and controlling person. Consequently, I went to school with a chip on my shoulder and a bad attitude. Being embarrassed was a very big button for me. I always thought everyone else was the problem. I also became very sneaky and into instant gratification. I loved baseball growing up and didn't smoke or use drugs until I joined the military at age seventeen.

On August 10, 1973, I enlisted in Oakland and went to Fort

I was the primary pawn in the religious tug-of-war between Catholicism and the Jewish/Hebrew teachings.

Ord for basic training and AIT (advanced individual training) as a records clerk. I didn't do well in the army for two primary reasons: (a) I didn't like authority, and (b) I had a problem with this other concept the army had, called—you guessed it—discipline.

By the time I discharged, fortunately with my benefits, in 1975, I had discovered drugs and it gradually progressed to my drug of choice, heroin. Within two years of discharging, I went to prison the first time when I was twenty-one.

I married on my twenty-fifth birthday to a great person and we had two daughters together, Nancy and Anna. They are twenty-three and twenty-one now and have children of their own, so I'm now a grandfather four times over.

I wasn't a good husband or father, as I lacked a lot of tools and information. I moved in 1981, divorced in 1986, and briefly remarried for another year and a half from 1987 to 1988.

Beginning in 1985, I started going in and out of prison on a frequent basis due to my escalated heroin use and the drug-seeking behavior associated with maintaining a habit. I did the revolving-prison thing for approximately seven years and was out five times for approximately 150 days for a thirty-day vacation during this period.

In 1991, in lieu of yet another prison term, I went to the Delancey Street Foundation, a two-to-four-year reeducational, relearning program for ex-offenders, addicts, prostitutes and/or homeless persons headquartered in San Francisco. I initially planned to stay only nine days until the day after Christmas, so I could go on a drug run, shoplifting and returning the merchandise for drug money. I messed up that plan and stayed five years. It not only was the hardest thing I've ever done, but also the most enriching experience of my life.

I did well for a while after graduating in 1996. However, I've been back in my addiction and beginning to experience problems again living in my addiction in the Tenderloin. Now I'm back in the county jail system.

KEITH STEIMLE

Life Story

It all started on March 28, 1981. I was born a third child, second son, youngest of all. All I remember of my life as a child was abuse from my father, not only towards me, but also towards my mother and my older brother, even though the only reason my older brother was ever beaten was for protecting us. Then my mother wised up and left the Bastard (my father) and took us kids. That stopped her from getting beat on for a while, except when the Bastard decided to come to our new house and beat on us, but I still got a three-day weekend of beatings every other weekend. Then my mother found another man who showed her nothing but love and he died of a heart attack when I was ten.

Well, the next three years were hell for me. This was the age of choices. The Bastard (my father) would lay out half a boat paddle, an extension cord, and a diesel truck wrench and let me choose which I got beat with. I chose the wrench and never cried until I locked myself in my bedroom. I was afraid if he saw tears that it would feed the fire.

On Christmas Eve of my thirteenth year the Bastard died. He was shot in the face by a rival biker with a twelve-gauge and I was called in to identify the body. About two weeks later, he was put into the ground. Through all of this I didn't cry. As a matter of fact, I thought I felt a smile at the funeral.

During all of this time my mother found another man. He too was a beater who beat on my mother and me for the next two years until one day I came in from playing Home Run Derby with my friends and he had her pinned on the floor choking her with one hand and about to punch her in the face with the other. All I saw was red and I beat him with the bat. I released fifteen years of beating, of hate, pain, anger, and rage, all at once and all on him.

Then my mother wised up and left the Bastard (my father) and took us kids. That stopped her from getting beat on for a while, except when the Bastard decided to come to our new house and beat on us

I told my mother to choose him or me and she did, she chose him, and told me to pack up and get out.

I truly wanted to kill him but my mother stopped me after about four minutes. I told my mother to choose him or me and she did, she chose him, and told me to pack up and get out. So I packed my things into my school backpack and on my way out I kicked him once more and told him if I ever saw him again that I was going to kill him and I meant it.

After that it was off to the real world and the world of doing drugs, learning to cook meth, hitchhiking around the country, and running from my problems.

I have been in and out of jail and juvenile for about ten years now. Now I am in another state and another jail, but this is the first time I have been arrested and feel I don't deserve to be. I sold two bags of weed to feed my dog, the only friend I have. He has been with me for fifteen months now and has saved my life twice—once from a man with a knife and once from a coyote that was within fifteen feet of biting me. I cried myself to sleep that night for the first time in seven years or more. As I cried, my dog, whose head is as big as mine, pushed his head against mine as if to say, it's okay, Toast, no one will hurt you again, so I vowed the same to him.

KEITH STEIMLE

Me and My Masks

The masked man is me, quiet, yet secure
The masks I wear change me, of that you can be sure
When I am insulted the mask I wear is hard
And sometimes I wear the dealer mask as I sell my shards
If I steal your Lexus to take it for a cruise
Or jack you for your wallet a ski mask might be used
When I need a lady, captain save-a-ho will suffice
But in front of that girl's mother I wear the one that's nice
If I'm in the club and see some honey looking sweet

I'll put on my player mask and they'll be begging at my feet
If their boyfriends see this, I'll take them to the street
And put on my Rocky mask, then their asses I will beat
If I wear my dope fiend mask just turn around and run
'Cause if I'm wearing this mask I could have a gun
But when I think about it, the mask I wear the most
Is the mask I like best, the mask that
I call Toast.

AFROM HAGOS

Life Story

I am Afrom Tecle Hagos Gangul. I am from a country in East Africa called Eritrea. I have four sisters and I have one brother, who is younger than me. I am the oldest out of us. I have a happy mother and happy father (family).

I have been through a lot of stuff, let me start from the beginning. I am eighteen years old, I was born November 11, 1985. My family and I came out to the United States in 1990 because of war in the homeland. We stayed in Dallas, Texas for one year, then we moved to Alameda, California. I had fun out there. A lot of my childhood memories that I can remember were in Alameda. Some were good and some were bad.

Two and a half years later I moved to Oakland, California. That's where a lot of my negativity started. The negativity did not start because I was a bad person, it started because I was always in trouble with others because someone always had something to say that was negative about me because I was African and darker than a lot of people. This started all in the schools from elementary to about the eighth grade. I guess that has a lot to do with me committing crimes, all the anger and vengeance that I have been holding in, I would call that internal pain. It's probably one of the

someone always had something to say that was negative about me because I was African and darker than a lot of people.

big reasons that I started smoking weed and drinking alcohol.

I have been kind of living a false image. Everything I thought was cool really is so dumb and is totally the opposite of reality. Even though I have had these problems in my life, I am still a respectful individual, and I come from a respectful family.

I have had a lot of violence in my life, and I have acted in violent ways for a long time. I am not scared to tell nobody because I am a good person who is in the act of changing his life and will be successful.

That was the lifestyle I was living most of the time. It was brought to me, but I'm not here to justify, I'm here to be open-minded and soak in all knowledge.

回

NESTOR REYES

Life Story

We were altar boys.

I lived my life for thirty years and counting. I did a lot, some good, some bad. As a kid I was okay. From kindergarten to high school I was in a private Catholic school. Most would say I was a handful. I did a lot of mischiefs a Catholic schoolboy could. We were altar boys. Yes, we drank the wine. After Sunday service and on school days we sneaked to the convent to watch the nuns. My actions probably sent a couple of nuns into early menopause. But everything was innocent and fun.

Now fast-forward to the years 1995 to 2005. I was an adult. I worked in different jobs, from the army to a bar, for a travel agency; in different companies from here to Hawaii. I mingled with adults, made decisions and suffered consequences, had fun, got hurt.

But it's a whole different ball game now. The innocence is gone. I got married to and divorced a woman who I blamed for my misfortune. In reality, although she was difficult, it was my fault because I was in an adult relationship and I acted like a kid. I lost my daughter and I blamed a biased judge. But it's my fault because I did not fight enough. When it started getting hard I gave up and now my life is in shambles. I lived it with no direction, no purpose, and I used my failure as an excuse to live as a child in an adult life. And now it has led me here, dressed in orange and in jail.

I almost reverted back to my old ways and tried to blame it on the justice system. Although flawed, I'm just a number and one of the many they screwed. I tried to blame it on a snitch but I already knew he was a liar and a coward. The truth is, this is my fault too. I allowed myself to mingle with weak people. I lived a code of silence that another world followed, where I didn't belong.

Now I'm treated like everybody else. My character is defined by the blue card my charges are written in. My identity is the jail number I wear on my wrist and again I'm insulted because I'm offered a deal for crimes that they can't prove, assuming I would take it. But they're wrong.

The irony of my life is that for twenty-nine years I lived like a child. When I turned thirty I was behind bars. When that day came, I became a man and, as a man, I would fight. I won't let them take years of my life. And like with all fights, there's a risk I might lose. Then I'll take comfort and say to myself, Welcome to adulthood.

*I lived a code of silence that another world followed, where I didn't belong.
Now I'm treated like everybody else. My character is defined by the blue card my charges are written in. My identity is the jail number I wear on my wrist*

DWIGHT YOUNG

Appointment with Death

I remember a time when I once
escaped my last breath, I was
being chased down by bullets
and my destination was death.

All I could do was run
and try to stop the inevitable

*I caught a /
glimpse of a red
river of souls.*

from happening and as I watched
day turn into night within a couple
of seconds my life started
flashing.

I envisioned images from
the cradle and then end in
the grave, I seen my life stuck
in prison, condemned as a slave.

I seen my daughter crying over
me saying, Daddy, don't go. And
at the same time I caught a
glimpse of a red river of souls.

I'm telling all this because it is
an actual fact I woke up
in the ER just for the doctor
to tell me, Welcome back
to the living.

MARGO PERIN

Welfare

Every Sunday at breakfast my father listened to Alistair Cooke delivering his *Letter from America* broadcasts on the radio. The cramped dining room was only big enough for a table to fit us all, with hard wooden chairs and a vaguely light-brown carpet underneath. The cream-colored wallpaper rippled slightly on the walls, as if it had been there since before World War II, and the small flowers lent an air of nostalgia to the cloud of depression that hung over us. The small bay window leaked in gray light from the low skies, and every so often a gust of wind rattled the glass.

Even though the chill in the air was palpable, the room was stifling. My father insisted on keeping the doors in the house shut as if they were chapters of his life he had closed for good. In his eyes, the past was only good for one thing: forgetting.

My mother sat forward in her chair at the foot of the table and twitched nervously. Her smudged eyes were on us but they were blank. She had gained weight since we had moved to Scotland and her dyed black hair puffed like a nest around her face. My siblings and I fidgeted and swallowed our cereal quickly, walled in by the threat that my father might hold a conference in the living room, where he'd line us up on the couch and hit us one by one.

Alistair Cooke's melodious voice rippled through the tense air. "Today President Johnson is facing one of the most important decisions of his presidency—"

My father cocked his ear as he poured his black coffee from one cup to another to cool it. Every so often his lips tightened and he blinked several times as if he were deep in thought.

"Dad," said Max innocently, breaking the silence with his as-yet-unbroken voice. He was still in his pajamas and had sleep in his eyes. "Why did we have to leave New York?"

"Be quiet," my father said. "I'm listening to the radio."

"But why, Dad?" Max's voice grew insistent. "Why do you keep making us move?"

"I said be quiet!" my father snapped.

Max flushed. "But Dad, I was only asking," he complained. "I'm sick of always having to go to a new school."

My father sighed exaggeratedly, then looked at him and said in a reasonable voice, "You wouldn't want your mother to go on welfare, would you?"

"Why would she have to go on welfare?" Ava asked, looking mystified. She had circled her eyes in kohl underneath white eyeshadow, just like her hippie friends had done when we lived in New York.

My mother sat forward in her chair at the foot of the table and twitched nervously.

My father swirled around and said sharply, "Who was talking to you?"

Ava buttoned her lips and put her head back down.

Max burst into tears and yelled, "It's not fair! Why do we have to keep on changing schools? Why do you make us move all the time?"

With the vein in his neck pulsing, my father stood up and reached towards Max to slap his face. "How dare you question me? Who do you think you are?"

Max leapt to his feet, tipping his chair over. "You're not going to hit me!" he sobbed. He flung open the door and raced out of the house. My father made a strangled sound and ran after him.

It was pouring outside. Through the window I could see my father chase my brother on the sopping wet and slippery grass with his arm outstretched to rein him in. Max skidded and fell down. Then he was up again and just escaped my father's grasp by weaving through the hedges that must have been neatly trimmed by the previous inhabitants. Finally my father caught him by the scruff of his neck. Twisting the collar of Max's pajama top with one hand, and using his other hand for balance, my father kicked him back into the house.

Through the open door, white-faced and silent, we could see my father bounce him up the stairs to his room, toe to butt, while Max screamed at the top of his voice.

That Max had almost died two years earlier in a car accident must have been another of my father's closed chapters, just one more thing he couldn't remember.

I made friends with a girl at school and one day, when we were in the park, I stepped barefoot on a broken bottle.

"Oh, for God's sake," said my mother when I arrived home at dinnertime with a deep gash in my toe. She gave me some aspirin and I wrapped a washcloth around it but it kept on bleeding. My father was in a good mood, warm from the couple of glasses of whiskey he'd had before dinner. "Let's get someone to look at that," he said jovially when I bent my head down and started crying. "Get your coat, we'll go to the emergency room."

The drive leading up to the hospital was dark except for a sign placed underneath a weak street light. "Dead Slow," it read.

"Ha ha," my father joked as he rolled the car through the open gates. "I guess no one comes out of here alive."

I forced a laugh because he got mad when we didn't laugh at his jokes. Inside the swing doors, I hobbled after him down a pale-green-walled corridor to the emergency room, which was empty except for a woman with a boy next to her. His knee had a hole in it and leaked blood down his bare leg, which made a long streak of red on his white skin. Around the stiff chairs were makeshift screens that drank up the fluorescent lighting, draining the room of color.

In his gentlemanly way, my father waited for me to take a chair, then sat down beside me. He lit a cigarette and blew out two long streams of smoke through his nostrils. Then he leaned towards me confidentially. "The National Health Service is a great idea. When Max had his accident in Florida, they would hook him up to a machine every day to see if he was still alive."

I looked at him, surprised. So he did remember.

He continued, "Every morning, I would have to pay thirty-five dollars before the technician would attach the machine. One day, I didn't have the money." He paused to remove his handkerchief from his back pocket. He blew his nose with a loud honk, then refolded the handkerchief and replaced it in his back pocket. "You know what that SOB did when I told him I would pay him later? He started putting the machine away. He said I had to pay him first."

"What did you do, Dad?" I asked breathlessly, almost choking in my anxiety to get information out of him.

"I walked home." He paused with his eyes to the ceiling and blinked several times. "I believe I was crying."

He drew more smoke from his cigarette holder, then said, "Do you remember Mr. Rosenberg?"

"They lived around the corner from us," I said encouragingly.

The drive leading up to the hospital was dark except for a sign placed underneath a weak street light. "Dead Slow," it read.

"What did you do, Dad?"

*I guessed she
meant Jewish*

Mrs. Rosenberg thought I was cute until I peed on the wall outside her house. I had to go, but no one was in my house and I was too scared to ask to use their bathroom. Peering over her pink butterfly sunglasses as she came out of the house, Mrs. Rosenberg had asked, "Why are your shorts wet?"

"They're not wet," I said.

She paused, then told me to wait. A few seconds later, she came back out of the house with a towel and placed it on the backseat of her car. "You can get in now," she said.

On the way to our beach outing, my shorts dried and nothing was said. I never told my mother what had happened. But it didn't matter because she had already told me not to go over there.

"They're weird," she said.

I guessed she meant Jewish because of the way she had frowned when Mrs. Rosenberg had said what nice Jewish kids we were. Which we were, something I wouldn't find out until long after I had walked off the map my parents had drawn.

The sharp scent of antiseptic brought me back to the hospital. My father was clearing his throat, gravel cutting through the smooth salesman pitch. "Luckily, I ran into Mr. Rosenberg on the street. He asked me what was wrong. When I told him, he pulled out his wallet and gave me fifty dollars." My father smiled warmly. "Ever since then, I have sent him two hundred dollars a year to thank him."

"Why didn't you have any money?" I asked.

My father's eyes emptied of expression. "That's a good question," he answered.

I sat in silence, trying to figure out how I could get him to tell me more, like did Mr. Rosenberg know we were here in Scotland, three thousand miles and an ocean away from where we belonged. I didn't realize that sending money would mean my father's whereabouts could be traced by the postmarks, so that must have been another lie.

My father seemed to grow bored and he squinted through the windows at the black night with his jaw clenched. He had little bags under his eyes and stubble on his chin. His skin was no longer suntanned as in all the sunny places we had lived, but his scent was still determinedly Old Spice and his suit unrumpled and new. His fingers reached for a cigarette, which he lit with a flick of his gold cigarette lighter.

I felt worried all of a sudden, a thick pulse at the back of my throat. "Dad, nothing's going to happen to you, is it?" I said anxiously.

"Don't be ridiculous," he frowned, whirling smoke in my direction. "What are you talking about?"

I sat back, bitten by his quick anger. My eye caught the boy's and I shrugged. The boy didn't respond. Flushing, I watched the black hands of the clock. After sixteen minutes a nurse appeared from the far side of the room and called my name. My father stood up with me, then glanced in my direction. "Margo, I have to go back home to make a phone call. Here." He handed me a coin. "You can get the bus back." He strode out of the waiting room as if he had important business to attend to.

The nurse led me to a large room with a table in the middle and a naked lightbulb above it. A doctor was standing in the corner and he told me to lie on the table so he could look at my toe. "Aye, this will need a couple of stitches," he said. He smiled down at me. "Look at the wall and count to one hundred. I'll be through in no time."

I turned my face to the side, moaning as he gave me a tetanus shot and then began to sew up my toe. The light threw shadows on the wall, magnifying his movements. Tears sprouted from my eyes as I watched, partly fascinated and partly sickened by the giant hand weaving up and down against the green paint. As he finished and wrapped my toe in gauze, I kept my eyes to the wall, blurrily transfixed.

"All right," he said, patting my leg. "You can get up now. We're through."

I let myself down gingerly and then stumbled through the waiting room out of the hospital and across the street to the bus stop.

As I waited for the bus, I was the only person on the dark empty street barely lit by a single streetlamp. A white sports car zoomed past. The brake lights flashed, and then the driver backed up with a loud rumble until he had pulled up next to me. "Do you want a lift?" the man asked, smiling across at me. A strand of his thin blond hair bounced on his forehead as he sized me up.

I shook my head, trying to look angry so he would go away.

"Come on, hen," he coaxed. "You'll have to wait ages for a bus."

"No, thanks," I said stiffly.

He moved in closer, resting his hand on the window ledge of the passenger seat. "Are you sure? I won't bite you."

I leaned my head to the side and squinted at him. "No, but do you have a light?" I said cockily. I pulled out a cigarette my friend had given me.

He laughed. "Aye, here you are." I leaned closer, breathing in when his flame flickered at the tip of my cigarette. Then I jerked back before he could pull me into the car. "Thanks."

"Are you sure?" he said.

"Yes," I answered, partly flirting, partly scared.

The man seemed bemused, and rode off.

I puffed on my cigarette, feeling proud of myself, and that I was pretty. The bus finally came, way after I'd smoked the cigarette down into the filter. It let me off on my street and I limped down the road to our corner. One street up squatted a small block of flats. Its bumpy concrete surface loomed in the dark, and outside on the small patch of grass was a man walking a large dog. He stood smoking a cigarette, watching his dog lift its leg and pee against a rubbish bin. The dog looked up as I hobbled by. Its eyes were dark as it stared at me, and I stared back. Without warning it leaped up and jumped on me, knocking me down. I screamed and pushed its suffocating hot belly as hard as I could but I couldn't get it off me.

"Charlie, heel!" The man whistled and the dog jumped off just as suddenly, then hovered beside me, growling.

I rolled over and staggered to my feet. "You should watch your fucking dog!" I screamed.

"There's no need to swear," said the man in a mild voice. "You should never stare at dogs, especially German Shepherds, don't you know that?"

"Fuck off," I said, limping away. When I arrived home, the hall light was casting a ghostly light onto the gravel. I staggered across the threshold, then wobbled upstairs. I passed my parents' bedroom on the way to mine at the back of the house. A thin ray of light shone underneath their door and I could hear the smooth sound of my father's voice inside and my mother's fainter one answering him, but the door was closed against me.

A thin ray of light shone underneath their door

Where I'm From

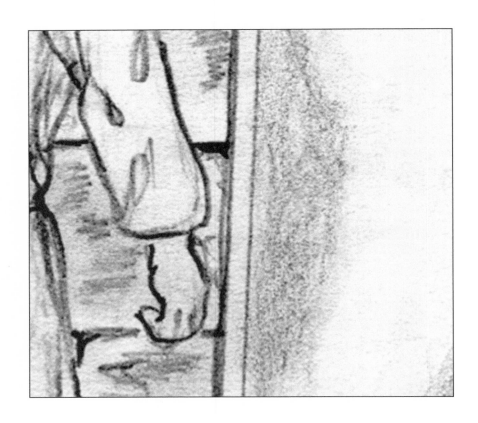

Some of the places I've been you'll never get there.
—John Martel aka Indio

回

OLLIS FLAKES

Coulda Been Me

This morning Dennis Richmond
Blurs on alert a double homicide
In a 'hood where I hang, two people
Had died
On Eddy and Scott someone's son
Was shot dead in the street
In the wee hours of the morning,
He shoulda been home asleep
'N' not even a mile away on
Golden Gate and Lyon
And probably less than an hour later
Someone else was dying

Sitting back to think about
This issue in silence
Capturing with pencil upon paper
A city infected by violence
So as I place myself
In my mind on the corner of Scott
Settling upon a place
Not far from where this brother got shot
I can sorta picture a man
Of middle age walking towards Eddy
In a place where I hang
On a street where I be
I figured, this coulda been me!

I figured, this coulda been me!

This here brother that's walking
Probably not knowing
He's becoming the victim
Of a predator stalking
Now, was there ever a chance
Of warning this brother to run?
Before the last sound he hears
Would be the blast of a gun
Or for the brother resting in
Peace down on Lyon 'n' Golden Gate
Who probably didn't realize then
That his time was too late
Or who probably didn't even stop to think that
Today he might meet his fate
Becoming another statistic
Of somebody's hate
But wait!

Things seemed different
As I laid on the concrete
Staring into the eyes of my killa
Who was standing on the street
'N' the first thing I thought was,
"Damn, this brother looks like me!"
But I guess I'll never know
As I fade into eternity
Now, 'fore this to be my last morning
I never woulda thought
That I'd pass without knowing if
My killa's been caught

As the blood spilled from my body
I looked towards the skies
Then the breath left my lungs

And I closed my eyes
Still cogitating in silence
I observed the death of the two brothers
Feeling the pain of their loved ones
Hearing the cries of their mothers
So before I began to write about my feelings
I turned off the TV
And the first thing I thought was,
"Damn, that coulda been me!"

JOHN MARTEL AKA INDIO

Oh, the Places You'll Go

Oh, the places you'll go is probably the places I've been. Some of the places are hot and dry. Some are cool and wet. Others are full of green meadows with colorful flowers filling the air with a scent of heavenly bliss.

Some of the places I've been smell like piss. They are dark and dirty, with people everywhere trying to get somewhere. They come in all shapes and colors and sizes, some are even in disguises. You see kids running around. You see drug needles on the playground. You see women with short dresses on with knee-high boots walking the street, sometimes until sunrise or they might get beat.

Sometimes you'll go to the edge of the earth to see the sunset. Maybe you'll go to the desert to see the lights at night. Hopefully you'll get down south and get on a big ride. You'll probably close your eyes and scream, but I'll advise you to hold on tight. You may even go underground to explore in caves, tunnels, or caverns. And in the same state towards the end of summer, the sky is full of colored balloons in different patterns.

Oh, the places you'll go will probably be the places I won't. Like

Oh, the places you'll go will probably be the places I won't.

a train ride in the autumn. Going through states like Pennsylvania, Virginia, North Carolina, and Kentucky. Watching the trees shed their colorful leaves. Oh, how I wish I could be so lucky.

So some of the places you'll travel you'll do it without me. Some of the places I've been you'll never get there. But all of these places have something in common. They're here for somebody from everywhere.

MICHAEL PAYTON

Where I'm From
(Inspired by Jay-Z)

I'm from the place where the church is the flakiest
Where people been praying to God for so long that
    they become atheist
I'm from the place where they call the cops the A-team
'cause they hop out of vans and spray things
I'm from the place where life expectancy's so low,
    we making out wills at FIFTEEN
I'm from a place where you smell piss in the hallways
You hear women yelling from domestic violence always
I'm from a place where the streetlights burn out
Old pimps permed out
Young girls turned out
I'm from a place where you got to keep one eye open like CBS
Where your friends become tedious
I'm from a place where we fight over blocks with buildings
    that make a killing
Where you got to be a sex offender or be killed for a
    news camera to come filming
A place where if the narks hit

We swallow spits
And if it's worth it, we pay a fiend to dig through our shit
I grew up and was raised all around this town
But I wouldn't change my stomping grounds
Because I'm Fillmore bound
Where I'm from . . .

回

MICHAEL PAYTON

Summer

You ain't never seen a summer like this bakin' hot
  and you could see the smoke comin' up off of bodies
But they ain't sweating, they on the ground leaking and
  smoke is comin' from the fresh bullet holes in they body
People already knew most of these victims would be makin'
  they exit soon
"Damn! Half his head off," and, "Look at the size of that exit
  wound."
Me and Phil told y'all about that rain, but the sun dried that up
  and it don't just shine, it beams
"I can't wait till the Cow Palace gun show, so I can send a friend
  to go cop me one of them new infrared beams."
This summer won't be no kids riding on bicycles
And when it's hot out, you might think you hear a lot of people
  whistle
But ain't nobody happy, that's just the silencer on the pistol
Cops ain't coming around, too many false calls to the rollers
Fourth of July is near and we poppin' fireworks from June until
  October
All you find on the ground is popped firecrackers and bullet
  shells

Forget the weather, the block on broil because these kats bring
    the heat like they Satan himself
It's too hot for me, the Lord must've wanted me locked up
'Cause I ain't trying to be number forty-nine on the news to get
    boxed up.

回

Kristian Marine

Korean Airliner

Sometime in the fall of second grade there was news of a Russian jet shooting down a Korean airliner. All the passengers died—mostly South Koreans. As a child of six years I'm sure I felt something inside when I heard the news. I knew I was Korean. South Korean. I knew that the people who died looked like me. I wondered if my biological mother had been on the plane.

I stood behind the tree with some friends. I don't know what we were doing or how it came up but I asked them if they had heard the news about the Russians shooting down the Korean plane. I searched their faces for reactions—shock, sadness, offense—but I saw none of what I felt reflected in their blank expressions. I felt alone in my sadness. My people were not their people, though their people were my people.

"My mom was on that plane. My mom was on that plane," I said and began to cry. I knew it was a lie but that was not what I meant. I meant, "I want you guys to feel some sadness too so I won't be alone." I meant, "Something awful happened today and you guys don't even care."

回

I knew it was a lie but that was not what I meant. I meant, "I want you guys to feel some sadness too so I won't be alone."

DWIGHT YOUNG

Who's Next in Line?

Who's next in line
Could it be me?
I bet it was the same
question my ancestors asked
before their life was snatched
by the colored people's rope in the tree
dying, and crying, pleading
for a better way of life
asking God to take away the
struggle and burden from family
kids and wife.
But at the same time
anticipating peace in death

Who's next in line?
to be brutally beat
skull crushed in defeat
by the blows of hatred, body crumpled up
like a brown paper bag
left by the gutter leaking.
Just another unsolved mystery
due to police brutality in the streets
of Hunters Point.

Who's next in line?
to spend ample amount of years confined
serving time, for a crime you didn't even commit
Life without the possibility of parole.
Who's next in line, to die an unwanted death (could it be me)

*Just another
unsolved mystery*

*No. Don't sit on
the front of this
bus. / No. Don't eat
at this restaurant. /
No. Don't drink
that water.*

THANE POUNCY

No!

No. Don't sit on the front of this bus.
No. Don't eat at this restaurant.
No. Don't drink that water.

No. You can't live here.
No. Don't no don't.

No. Don't come to this school.
No. Don't try to work here.

No. No. No.
No. You can't play at this park.
No. Don't be caught after dark.
No. No. No.
No. There ain't no future for you.
In this world.

Well, what do you think?
Did we listen?
No!

MARGO PERIN

Geography

There is a Native American expression, "You know who you are
when you know where you come from." If that is true, I will never

know who I am. My parents decided when I was a child that they would re-create themselves, to be without a past, or family, or culture, or religion. When I was seven my father got into trouble and my parents, six siblings and I began a life on the run, often moving in the middle of the night, always without warning. From then on we came from nowhere, defined by who we were not, not by who we were. My siblings and I didn't know what my father had done, or why we had to keep relocating. As we moved, so too did our internal landscapes, and our lives became a chain of shifting realities, linked by secrets and shaped by my father's growing violence and deceptions.

For the next seven years we moved eight times, covering five countries and two continents, ending up in England when I was fourteen. My name had changed and so had my face, my nose surgically altered in the attempt to hide my parents' Jewishness. I made my escape two years later, determined to be who I was and find the home I'd never had.

But I didn't know who I was, who my "people" were, or where I belonged. I was filled with the wounds of my childhood, confused about where I'd been and what had happened to me. Within a few years my life had crumbled. Like a war veteran, I was stuck in the war. Unless I went back to the battlefield and figured out what had happened, I would never be able to move forward.

So I began to write down everything I could remember. Somewhere at the back of my mind I recalled my father saying he'd been in the newspaper so I went to a library and examined microfiches of New York newspapers from the fifties and sixties and found him there. Then I went back and retraced my memories, step by step, charting the places, the years, the events, the people who suddenly turned up in our lives and disappeared again. I arranged the pieces like a jigsaw puzzle, then began shuffling them into sense, making shapes from what had been shapeless, bringing onstage what had been so meticulously concealed behind a curtain of lies.

As I collected, dissected and analyzed the facts from behind that curtain, the long forgotten call of place began to sound its lonely cry, like a whale stranded in the middle of the sea. All those countries where we lived had taken up residence in my cells, their geographies lurking in the map of my body, making up the continents, oceans and poles that have formed me. New York, where we began, is my heart and Mexico, the land of our first escape, my throat and chest. From Nassau grew my gut, and Florida the blood that courses through my body. Scotland pulses in my groin and London pounds the soles of my feet. Like a fetus, I grew that way, piece by piece.

Family

No nurturing from our parents leads us to seek it in other ways. Even jail nurtures what we need, when we need to be looked after, once comfortably used to it. County jail is Mommy and prison is Big Daddy.

—Edwin Armando Alvarez

OLLIS FLAKES

Ollis

This is the story of three different kinds
Of three different people
With three different minds
Although individuals, they're quite the same
Almost identical in appearance
Even sharing the same name
And that name is "Ollis"

As my dad's was before mine
Which now belongs to my son
Who's next down the line
Three generations, all rolled up in one
So, I begin this piece for Ollis Earl Flakes I
Cuz that's how the story began

Now, I really don't know too much about his childhood
But, what I do know, is that he lived his life good
I remember seeing photos of a teen
Horseback riding, swimming, fishing in a lake
For a championship title, winning a five thousand dollar stake

'N' at that moment if you could see his smile 'n' then look at
    mine

You would say to yourself that they're one of a kind
But he also faced problems, which most people often do
'N' a generation later I find myself haunted by these same
    problems too

'N' hopefully my son won't have to deal with this phase
Of being haunted by my problems as he grows old in his days
Cuz as a youngster watching my father deal with the struggle of
    a man
Not understanding what he did
But watching him make the best way that he can

But for some odd reason, he left when I was still an adolescent
Rolling a piece of my making without my dad in my presence
And I wonder if he faced the demons I may soon face
Splitting a father 'n' son relationship
Leaving it totally outta place

So I must look to the streets looking for my father
My figure, my niggah
Fighting the same addictive problems I once watched him battle
Against demons that were much more bigger
And at times I find myself lost
In a losing battle that I can't win

And upon reaching my adulthood, I was blessed with the
    presence of my father once again
But this time it was different, we were so much alike we hardly
    liked each other
The father figure I've searched for so many years in the street
Seemed to remind me of my older brother
We looked alike, we dressed alike,
Causing confusion with our mirrorlike reflection
It was like hanging out with some niggah that I hung out with on
    the street

So I must look to the streets looking for my father / My figure, my niggah

'N' not a father who'd offer any sense of direction

So, for a year we went through this misguided shit
I felt somewhere down the line that this shit had to quit
So I packed my bags 'n' said my farewells
'N' once again, father 'n' son had made a split
Separated,
And this time forever

Gone in the blink of an eye with many questions left unanswered
And me never knowing the reasons why
You were never around to feel my pain
Or wash away the tears I cry
Which has left me with a sense of feeling guilty towards self
Cuz I never got to say good-bye

*now I have my own
son / Naming him
after myself / As you
had once done*

'N' not only that, now I have my own son
Naming him after myself
As you had once done
'N' when I look at him it gives me a lift
To have become a father 'n' having to share that gift
'N' I cherish the ability to show him the things that I never
    learned from you
So help me become the father figure he needs
Giving direction to the things he's learning to do

I see you in him in so many ways
In the way he smiles, and in the jokes he plays
And he's just as athletic as the both of us in his adolescent phase
Every now 'n' then he may get under my skin, and even on my
    nerves as I done you back then
But for the most part he's a good little fellow, I love him to death
Because without you, Ollis is all I have left.

The Park

My happiest time was spent in a park
I remember her smile
As I push her on the swing
Wheeee . . . Daddy, again, she would shout
After she got tired of the swing
She would tirelessly climb up and down
On the slide
While I waited and watched
As she slid
Careful, Ella, I would shout
Then both of us would terrorize the pigeons
Throw bread then chase them and watch them fly
My baby had so much energy
She had fun
She smiled
She was me
Then we would lay on the grass and point at the sky
I put her on my chest and pretended to fly
Then we would walk home hand in hand
Before going home we'd go to Foodland
And come out with an ice cream in her hand
I haven't seen her for three years now
How could I bear not to go back
What kind of dad did she have
In my heart I have so much hurt
All I want is to go back to the way it was
When me and Ella played in the park

*All I want is to go
back to the way
it was*

*I was about eleven
years of age and
sitting next to a lady
on a crowded bus.*

R. L. LOVE

Dissertation of a Thief

I was about eleven years of age and sitting next to a lady on a crowded bus. I crossed my arms and with my left hand, in a slow pensive manner, lifted her coin purse from the loose sweater pocket. Using my right arm as a shield, I brought the coin purse to my left side and emptied it into my left jacket pocket. Nearing my designated bus stop—I had to hurry—I snapped the coin purse closed and returned it to her pocket. At that age, the most amazing part to me was she'd never know it was me, because, after all, I didn't take all her change, and two, she still had her coin purse.

So in years that followed, a crowded bus did not intimidate my behavior. Neither did an occupied dwelling or a busy street. Always neat, always quiet, always with consideration . . . You see, whether a home or business, I'd never take all the money or jewelry, and wallets would find a way to a nearby mailbox. Always warm adrenaline gave me the courage I needed. Always methodical and tidy with delicate concentration—this may have contributed to never getting caught. Later I wondered about my unusual manner to pickpocket, and soon enough I realized that maybe I was the mirror image of something I was taught.

At a very young age I walked down the hall to pass my parents' room. From my peripheral vision I observed my mother lifting my father's wallet from his pants pocket. In the dim shade-drawn room he slept in a minute snore of pleasure; for he was a longshoreman who worked at night and collected slumber during the day. Her fingers coordinated and agile, she removed a few bills of currency, closed the wallet, and replaced it in a methodical and tidy manner (through my youth she did this many times and never was ever caught—at least not by my dad). A surreptitious glance over her shoulder found me rooted in the doorway. She waved me away with her hand and a serious stern look; I was not included in her plans.

We studied one another until I drifted away, taking with me no realization of what a responsible adult had taught her child—

perhaps another part of life I had never seen, but would somehow later live.

Today I understand how her unusual self-reliance may have been necessary in many different ways, and I realize the contrast created a divorced mother and a drug-alcohol-jail-prison-hospital-bound son.

Do I love my mom? Would "no" be out of proportion with life? Or should I say "yes" and let you believe a mystery? Either way, my mom and I still have this bond and I am not so emotionally alone.

Or should I say "yes" and let you believe a mystery?

Today I want to question her, tell her what manifested and feel how she reacts. No blame, no judgment . . . for today I understand the self-reliance of her own survival.

MICHAEL PAYTON

Dear Mom

I know it was hard raising a kid like me
Especially with four other kids who was just as bad as me
But I was the outcast, born in the middle
Two older and two younger, three different dads, I knew two of
    them but mine and my sister's dad was a riddle
No man around the house to show me the other route
Me being the oldest boy, made me wanna run the house
My big cousins was selling dope and it kept them dressed clean
Pops never did shit but tried to call me once when I was thirteen
I took the phone from you, hung up and never spoke
It was hard being twelve on welfare needing school clothes
My cousin Turtle-T fronted me a sack
At that age was when I found out you smoked crack
I don't know what hurt me more, me finding out or my cousin
    selling it to you

It was hard being twelve on welfare needing school clothes

*You relapsed
twice but the third
program made the
whole family go
together*

And it hurt me more when my friends was visiting playing
    Nintendo smelling it too
I couldn't blame my cousins, I sold it to my friends' mothers too
That was just a part of that game that I never knew
Two years passed, I'm getting older now
My aunt Ruby passed, but you not slowing down
You caught two cases and the CPS was getting in your business
The family was talking, saying Loyce can't handle her children
I was damn near on my own, but I loved school
The sports, the girls, and the money I made from selling dope
    had me dressing cool
Broken promises, is what you gave me
Until I was sixteen and you went to the rehab, you never raised
    me
I don't know what it did but that program made you better
You relapsed twice but the third program made the whole family
    go together
That was the one, the one that changed our life
We went from eating EOC boxes of honey sandwiches to
    shopping at Safeway overnight
I still rebelled for those lost years
Started getting into fights at school, just to hide my tears
At the age of eighteen, I caught my first case
Turtle taught me well, but he never taught me about this place
In and out after that, the police knew my name
I started selling weed, I had to change the game
I was supposed to be a real man now, but making boyish
    mistakes
At the age of twenty selling weed out your house, got you kicked
    out your new place
And when I called you and you said that everything would be
    alright
That was the first time I sat in jail and cried
MAMA LOVED ME, POPS LEFT ME
Since that day I've been apologizing indirectly

You've been through it all, you a strong woman
That's why just like you is how I want my own woman
I know I don't say it much, but Moms, I love you
I've been buying you all those things to make it up to you
Paying phone bills sometimes even paying rent
Even though I don't stay with you and not that much time is
    spent
When we do talk and chill, I know all of this was meant
MAMA RAISED ME AND I WAS LUCKY
Mom, all we've been through, you must've loved me.

回

SHARON THOMAS

News from Home

I'm an only child
And sometimes I feel so lonely
No, I mean alone
No, I mean unloved
Maybe uncared for
Or maybe forgotten
But I was truly surprised the other day
When I received
A letter from my daughter
She expressed how much
She loved
Missed
And needed me
In her life
It made me feel whole
And then to put the icing on the cake
I phoned my mother
Only to be informed that

*I'm an only child /
And sometimes I feel
so lonely*

My son had been pursuing a music career
And was on the BET network
He had also called to say
That his goal was to provide and
Take care of his son and myself
This news makes me feel so good and complete
So wonderful
So loved

TIMOTHY HECK

Laundry Day

I'm not telling this story for sympathy, I'm not telling it to excuse anything I've done, and I'm certainly not saying that I have it worse than anybody else. There might not be anything interesting about this story at all, but for some reason, it stands out in my mind.

A lot of details have been lost or forgotten but I'm still going to tell you what I remember. I'm not sure how old I was when it happened but I was young, maybe ten or eleven, and my brother was only a couple of years older than me. It had to have happened on a Sunday. Because Sundays were the days our mom always set aside for the household chores. Neither of us had any chores in particular so the work was always left up to our mother's discretion. Because of my and my brother's laziness, we were always at odds with Sundays. Usually she wanted us to do something endless like pulling weeds in the garden she never planted flowers in, or laundry. My dad always found some excuse to leave the house on Sunday, can't say I blame him.

On this particular Sunday my brother was given the laundry job.

On this particular Sunday my brother was given the laundry job. I don't remember what my job was, I guess because it wasn't important. What is important in this story is my brother and his job. The laundry wouldn't have been so bad if only we had a dryer, but we didn't. So my brother had to carry these heavy loads of hot soaking wet clothes into the backyard and hang the laundry one by one and start over until it was done.

Anyway, he did as he was told until the last load. What happened was my brother didn't have enough for a full load of his own laundry so my mom had him wash some of mine with his. That pissed him off 'cause he hated doing anything for me. After washing everything, he hung his clothes out to dry, leaving mine in the washer to collect mildew.

I didn't find out about my clothes being left in the washer until way later that night. I don't remember how I found out but right after that is when the details begin to come to mind.

First, I remember feeling hurt and wondering why he would do that to me. I didn't do anything to him, at least not lately. Now, I easily could have added some more clothes, started the load over, and dried them in the house, but I didn't. Instead I told Mom, and that was my mistake.

The issue was petty, or at least it should have been. Right away our mom called him out and began to yell at him, telling him how stupid and lazy he was. I remember feeling satisfied, like justice was being served. I was almost proud of myself.

Just as my standing there had gotten awkward, our mom told me to go finish the laundry. I wasted no time. By the time I had gotten back from the laundry room, my brother was at the end of his rope and had started yelling back. This had never happened before. I think I was more surprised than she was.

He went on to tell her how sick and tired he was of always being treated like her slave rather than her son. Only he didn't just tell her, he shouted it at her. To an extent he was right but his style and timing was way off.

I tried to sneak out the room but I was spotted. She snapped at me to stop and I froze. Turning her focus back at my brother she jumped at him with a "how dare you" ferocity. She had a thin leather belt in her right hand raised above her head.

Before she touched him, he dropped to the ground into the fetal

I told Mom, and that was my mistake.

Like I said, there's nothing interesting about this story. I'm not even sure why I told it to you. I guess it just had to be told.

position. I remember the sound of the belt slicing the air, followed by the cold hard smacking sound of leather to flesh. She continued to whip him between words . . . DON'T-YOU-EVER . . . !

When his screaming got too loud, she stopped, and then continued. I remember suddenly feeling responsible for what I was watching, twitching with each sound. I remember feeling like it was me she was beating, or maybe that it should have been me. Why was I watching this? What was my lesson? She beat him until blood began to pour from the welts on his back and arms. I remember not getting any sleep that night. I don't have to guess that neither did he.

Like I said, there's nothing interesting about this story. I'm not even sure why I told it to you. I guess it just had to be told.

TIMOTHY HECK

The Visit

The visit was only an hour long. She was dressed casual and had only brought a black shawl to keep her warm, it was over 100° in AZ when she left and didn't think it was going to be that cold here in California. That was funny for me 'cause when I was younger she never let me leave the house without a jacket, you know, just in case. When she came in the visiting room she almost passed me by. As she sat down she pressed her hand against the window and I did the same. I already had the phone receiver in my hand and pressed against my ear, she just sat there for a second staring at me, not staring into my eyes but staring at me savoring the moment. When our eyes met I broke into a huge smile and then noticed her eyes become red like they do just before an onslaught of tears. Everything I wanted to tell her was just spinning through my head until the moment she picked up the phone . . .

TIMOTHY HECK

Untitled

Every time you hit me you did two things.
You drew me closer to you,
And pushed me further from myself.
I wanted to love you
I tried so hard
I even began to act like you,
Think like you,
Talk like you,
And even punish myself the way you punished me.
I would kill myself to prove my love.
No matter where I'm at
I can feel your phantom grip on my soul,
Like a guiding force
From my childhood.
I am unworthy of your love.
Please forgive my weakness
And release me from this torture.
Let me find myself
And live my life.

Every time you hit me you did two things. / You drew me closer to you, / And pushed me further from myself.

ERNEST FISHER

Rites of Passage

I went to see Dad in Hood River, Oregon, about twenty miles from the bottom of Mount Hood. I had some great times up there, hiking through the woods, picking blackberries, raspberries and strawberries

*now was going to be
the true test*

in the summer, saving my money in my own bank account. I hadn't seen my brothers and sisters for two years. I was going to be twelve this year. I felt like I was a man, for going hunting with my father was a huge stepping stone in the ranks of becoming a man between my siblings and me. Earlier in life I outshot all my brothers in marksmanship down at our local firing range but now was going to be the true test.

We went up into the forest between Hood River and Mount Hood, taking the same trails we used to go with the chainsaw to gather firewood. I had my Winchester and I remember feeling like Daniel Boone or a big-game hunter like Teddy Roosevelt from history class. There were pine needles all over the ground and you could smell the morning dew on them. It was my first hunting trip with the big boys so according to the rule of rites of passage I got the lead, or scout, position. I had been squirrel hunting and jackrabbit hunting before as well as pheasant, but besides wild boar, this was the true test of the hunger to get an elk or deer. My eldest brother got a six-point buck and so far my other two older brothers hadn't gotten any. In my mind I knew if I got one, in my father's eyes I would be raised into the honor position. I was hoping above hope that this would be my lucky day, that all the stars would be lined up in favor of me. I was hoping for a star all my own like Jesus had.

I went ahead of the pack, trying not to make any noise, going into the wind so the deer couldn't smell me coming. I had great expectations that just over the next hill would be Iron Star, a buck that got away three years back. I had been hearing about this buck for two months now, ever since I got to Oregon, and I just knew I was going to be the one. My brothers seemed to be making a lot of noise on purpose; none of my brothers wanted a twelve-year-old snotnose to outdo them. The sun was just coming up, the sky going from azure to light blue, the air crisp, with winter only two months away. It was beautiful country, with views of Mount Hood one way, with its majestic peaks and snowy white-haired top showing the wisdom of ages past, and the valley below with the different pines intermingled with oak, walnut and elm trees. Way off in the distance you could see the river that separates Oregon and Washington. I came across some tracks and deer droppings and by the size of them we knew it was a buck. I was now sure I was going to get Iron Star.

I started moving faster, not wanting old Iron Star to get away. My heart was like thunder in my ears. It was a little hard to breathe, this was really living. I was alive, charged with the excitement of the moment. I thought I could smell this mighty stud. Dad said Iron Star was at least thirteen points, maybe more. I thought my dad looked at me with a smirk; I thought he knew I was going to get my buck.

Three hours went by with no luck. We came by some bear tracks and now I had a little fear, not only because I didn't want to come across a bear, but also I was a little worried that the bear might have eaten my buck. We stopped for lunch and we started heading back the other way. My hopes drowned, feeling the feeling of failure coming home empty-handed.

I'm now the last one in line, feeling lower than the blue belly of a lizard. Somehow my older brothers and father got about two hundred yards ahead of me. I had stopped to go to the bathroom. As I was trying to catch up I came around the bushes and less than five yards in front of me there was Iron Star. I couldn't breathe. This buck was huge, beautiful, a white chest and chestnut to brown in color, huge eyes and at least fifteen points. Its nose was flaring because of my smell.

All of a sudden the buck jumped and in my direction. I jumped backwards, tripping over some shrubs or roots. As I fell my rifle shot off, going through the neck of this beautiful beast, killing it instantly. My father and brother were yelling out my name, running back to find me with this deer. My brothers couldn't believe what they were seeing and admiration and jealousy were fighting in their emotions.

Dad looked at me with wonder but also with a look that all boys like to see in their father's eyes. Dad was proud to be my father. At

My hopes drowned, feeling the feeling of failure coming home empty-handed.

that moment I wish I could have basked in that. I wasn't going to tell anyone and blow it. But I was sick to my stomach for killing the deer. I thought it was looking at me asking me, Why did you kill me?

I was trying to enjoy the hero's moment but I kept looking back at Iron Star and I just knew he blamed me for his predicament. When we went home I began to feel trepidation for I knew what was going to happen once we got there. As we got the deer off the hood of the truck, Dad hooked the hooves of the deer in a rope to raise it over the tree branch. Next he slit Iron Star's throat and the gravity started draining the blood. Dad called me over and rubbed the blood all over my face and hair. I almost retched right then and there. Dad then skinned the beast, cutting up the meat. Although I was sick because of the blood, I had no reservations about eating old Iron Star for dinner once he was cooked.

My dad still has the head and antlers hanging in his living room, seventeen points, a trophy I've never been proud of. I never did tell my dad and brothers that it was an accident killing that old buck.

GARY HARRELL

Family Tree

I began my first day of school only to find myself sitting on the corner down the street and around the corner from my house. I was crying, not knowing what to do. I was only just barely the age of six.

I sat there and cried and cried and cried. My heart was broken. Why? My thermos in my brand-new lunch pail was broke. My brother flipped the latch and there went my milk.

Shattered upon the sidewalk my thermos was smashed. I was so upset, I wanted to drink milk out of my thermos, not some stinking milk carton.

I got on this corner, crying. The lady who owned the house on the corner called the police, for she did not know what to do.

When the cop showed up he was baffled. What was he to do with a small child my age?

I wouldn't tell them who I was nor what was wrong.

The handcuffs were too large so he wrapped me in a blanket and off to the station I went.

I finally told them to call my grandmother who called my father. That was who finally came to my aid. I could only remember wanting to go to Grandma's house to eat cake and cookies.

LEONARD BOYLAND

This Is the Truth about My Mother and Why You Shouldn't Blame Them

My mother, whether in rebellion or out of lustful desires or because of love for a man, engaged in activities that impregnated her five separate times. And in all those possible life-threatening choices, not only to her but to her offspring, she gave birth and became mother to them all. Unbeknownst to me until about age fourteen was the fact that there was one before me that unfortunately didn't survive and I'm unclear as to when, what, how, or why, with the exception that my mother was not part of any reasons for his demise. She most certainly faced obstacles both internal with family and external with everything else.

Yet she raised us and the other three, one by rape and two by my stepfather, to a productive adult life filled with potential to accomplish any goal before us despite closed doors and closed minds. But most importantly, we all grew up to be unselfish, forgiving, and loving of each other and others among us. We were faced with many difficulties that would cause most to be bitter, isolated, and hateful, one being in a society full of racial discrimination,

The handcuffs were too large so he wrapped me in a blanket and off to the station I went.

segregation, and recrimination. Although some forms of negative behaviors and characteristics did develop she, through her values, qualities, and spiritual upbringing, insured that we developed those positive attributes even more so.

回

LEONARD BOYLAND

What's Wrong?

My mama sat there and cried. For the first time in my eight or nine year old life, I felt her pain of helplessness, her loss of hope, and her sense of despair. I already knew how to work and earn money. I understood that anything earned belonged to the family first as our obligation of being a member. Maybe that was the initial purpose for the endeavor to credit needed groceries, flatly refused, that caused the destitution and despair, but to no avail.

I wondered if her tears were for me or her. Were they because she could not protect me at such a young age from the cruelty of life and the society

I wondered if her tears were for me or her. Were they because she could not protect me at such a young age from the cruelty of life and the society we live in? The fact that spinning tops, shooting marbles, or climbing trees don't have anything to do with her harsh realities. The responsibilities of going to work, buying food and clothing, washing, cleaning hand-me-downs, and the all-important task of keeping a roof over our head, even though at times they were roach infested homes in mice or rat infested areas. And contrary to our child's perspective, it did not happen with the money picked off the ground or limbs of the trees on which it grows.

Or maybe her crying was because of the simple fact that between my daddy and her, it was impossible for us not to be affected by their inaccessible means to provide or care for us.

But for whatever the reason, her rising up after the fallen trees and freeing her growing baby to become a grown man renewed a lost hope that I will never lose again.

RANDY NICHOLS

Dear Janice, Dear Elmer, Dear Dad, Dear Joe, Dear Mom

Dear Janice,

. . . you were a beautiful young teenager of around eighteen or nineteen. You were our babysitter. Alls I remember is someone said, I'll show you my tits if I can see yours. You took off your top and served us lunch. After lunch you put Cory to bed and took Tammy and I into the living room and we all got naked. You played with my pee-pee and made it hard. Don't you remember how scared I was? Then you told me what I was supposed to do with it. When I said, Okay, can I do that to you, you said, No, do it to your sister. You had Tammy lie down on the carpet and spread her legs. You told me to lie on top of Tammy. I just knew that wasn't right, but I did as you told me. My skinny little body was shaking. You told me to put my pee-pee in my sister. Never have asked Tammy if she remembers this, I hope not. 'Course we've both been plagued with a troubled life . . .

you said, No, do it to your sister.

Dear Elmer,

. . . maybe I was eleven years old when I first laid eyes on that blue Ford pickup with the shotguns in the gun rack. I had just finished a slice of watermelon and a mug of root beer at the counter of your mom's fruit stand. Your mom was a wonderful lady, she was so proud of her son Elmer. Yeah, you saw the sparkle in my eye when I looked at your shotguns. I burst with joy when you pulled that pump shotgun down off the gun rack and said, Here, hold this. Wow, you knew your way right into a young boy's heart. You were much more different than the others, you were slower in your assault. You would give me gifts and take me hunting and camping. Then one day it happened. You grabbed my leg and started grooming me for your attack.

you knew your way right into a young boy's heart.

This went on for an extremely long time. Right into puberty. I lie back at times and remember some of those encounters, you taking me hunting and camping always to end with a sex act. The thing that has affected me the worst was you took something from me the others didn't. That was my rite of passage into manhood. You took me to Stockton to get laid the very first time by that prostitute Robin. I really thought that was cool, until you hid in the kitchen to watch, then when Robin went into the bathroom after finishing with me, you had me come into the kitchen to jack you off so you could save yourself twenty dollars, you cheap bastard. That simple act has caused me to feel inadequate my entire life. Every time I would attempt to be alone with a woman, I'd find myself looking through the room and in the closets to make sure someone wasn't hiding there . . .

Dear Dad,

. . . although you've been gone for eleven years, it seems like only yesterday that I was sitting in front of the window waiting for you to show up and take me fishing. Seems like I've been sitting in front of the window for thirty-five years. Dad, you left me so long ago, long before you died. I used to listen to you come home late at night and start fights with my mom. I used to comfort Tammy and Cory when you were tearing up the house, I knew you were hitting Mom, 'course she always defended you the next morning. You tried to blame Mom for the divorce. Why did you have to drink so much? You used to tell me I was a piece of shit and would never amount to anything. For a very long time, I believed that. You never knew about me being molested, you weren't around. What would have happened if you would have been there to protect me? You were never there for any of my Little League games. I was the only boy there without his dad. That used to hurt, then later I just became numb from it. I used to even try to defend you when I was a kid.

Later on in life I went into some of the very same bars you used to drink in. When they found out I was your son they would buy

You used to tell me I was a piece of shit and would never amount to anything. For a very long time, I believed that.

me a drink and tell me how great you always said I was and how proud you were of me. Funny, I don't remember it like that. Hell, you never told me you even loved me. I used to think, Why is he lying to these people, then I would really think how much of a disappointment I must have been that you had to tell lies.

I always told myself that I would never be like you. I'd always be there for my children and never beat on my wife. Well, Dad, you ought to be proud of me, I did become you. I'm a drunk and drug addict . . . As for my daughter Melissa, she's still sitting by the window waiting for me to take her fishing. She's been sitting there for about seventeen years . . .

Dear Joe,

. . . you were probably the worst type of predator I've encountered, simply because you hid your sickness behind being gay. In the beginning I really thought you were a kind and gentle man, only to be confronted with the truth of just how violent and perverted you were. Playing on my mother and father's problems just to build confidence and trust so you could one day brutally sexually attack me. You attempted and succeeded to take a large dick and insert it into a young boy's rectum. I've lived in pain, shame, embarrassment, and guilt every single day of my life. The worst part of this whole fucked-up event is you made me believe for many, many years that my mom knew about this sick perversion and that it was okay by her. Do you have any idea how a child eight or nine years old feels when he's made to believe his mom, let alone his father who abandoned him, doesn't care what happens?

All those years I've only felt pain, that's what I thought love was, a sea of pain. I really wish I knew where you were, how I could reach you, I would like to cause pain and grief in your life. However, I don't and I thank God I don't because I might not be able to hold my anger in and would undoubtedly spend the rest of my life in prison, of course I been here already a vast majority of my life.

It's been very hard over the years to not take out my anger and vengeance on other child molesters. Instead I've been destroying

that's what I thought love was, a sea of pain.

myself and my life by stabbing needles into my arms to not feel the pain you caused. To not to smell your breath I still smell, to not feel your dick inside my ass. To not feel your sweat on my backsides, to not hear your voice saying in my ear, Don't cry, Randy, it won't hurt long, to not see my mom's face as she tells me I have to go to your house. You bastard, you took more from me than my ass, you took my innocence, you took my mom from me.

It's over, one more to go . . .

Dear Mom,

I'm writing this in hopes of coming to terms with who Randy is and why Randy has done what he has done. But no way is this an attack on you or your character as my mother. You are my mother and I do love you deeply; however, I have harbored some very deep resentments for most of my life. Ever since I was five years old or so I've felt unwanted and abandoned—guess it stems from that time when I stole those caps and you forced me to take them back and stand there and feel fear, embarrassment, shame, and guilt. I shit my pants that day.

For the life of me, I couldn't figure out why my mommy did that to me. Over the next ten or twelve years, I felt let down by you, actually even longer, and I will write about it in this letter. I think of the embarrassment from your attempts to cut my hair and the butchered look I had after each of these attempts.

Mom, I never liked myself as a child growing up, don't know if you noticed or not. I didn't have many friends, being pigeon-toed and wearing black-framed glasses as a child didn't help matters much. I remember that board you always made me walk along to help my pigeon-toed problem. I also had to take that pill every day—Ritalin. I hated all these things. Hell, I remember almost getting held back in kindergarten. Dad rescued me then; however, the following year Dad wasn't around and then you let them keep me back in first grade.

Yeah, four-eyed freak that took pills, walked funny, and who was stupid too. That's how I viewed myself, of course that's how I was viewed by the kids around me too.

Naturally, when I was molested each time I felt unloved because you were there, but you weren't. Mom, as time grew on, I felt we grew further apart. You would work all day, then go partying at night. I guess you did the best you could—a single mother raising three kids on minimum wage; just the same, something was missing.

There was an extremely tremendous amount of incidents that happened to me as a kid that you don't even know what happened, you weren't there.

The divorce played a major roll in my self-destructiveness and really plagued me for years. Then after I grew up, got married, had Melissa, and got in trouble, you were there to pick up the self-destruction and raise my daughter. You did a wonderful job with her; however, that bothers me. Why couldn't I get the same treatment when I grew up, why couldn't I be protected from the world's predators? I'm glad you were there for her, I'm just jealous you weren't there for me. Then later in life it seemed useless to try to become close to Melissa, it was obvious that I wasn't ever going to get to raise her. My excuse was, I couldn't take her from you, but hey, you took her from me, or maybe you saved her from me.

I don't know, Mom, seems there's a lot more to say but the pain right now is too deep to go to. Besides, I don't want to hurt you, I just want to express what I don't feel I ever had and that's a supportive mother.

Anyhow, please take care and I'll write more soon.

Love, Randy—the one who made you Mom first.

four-eyed freak that took pills, walked funny, and who was stupid too. That's how I viewed myself, of course that's how I was viewed by the kids around me too.

why couldn't I be protected from the world's predators?

*For some reason I
look in the mirror . . .
it was the first time
I saw shame and
abandonment*

R. L. LOVE

The Kiss

In 1965, at the age of nine, I remember my mom's sisters came to visit from L.A. The Voices—that's what I called my aunts because of the constant chatter—were talking about my cousin and how he had been admitted to the military hospital . . . something about how a doctor was going to amputate his leg. One day I was able to visit him, but I had to stay outside and wave to him from a very small garden next to the hospital window. After his operation, a short period passed and he came to live with us.

My two brothers and I shared the same room, and they slept together while I had a bed to myself—so that dictated that my cousin would share my bed. One night a vague and distant confusion would capture my adolescent spirit. Somewhere late into that night he moved his body behind me, pulled my underwear down, and began his selfish rhythm that diminished my awe of him. Trembling deep in my abdomen, I felt his hot foul breath on my neck until his erection spewed something wet on my lower back. Passive fear captivated me as I realized . . . there is, there has to be, a bogeyman . . . he's breathing on my neck. Finally done, his orgasm sufficient, he said, "Go wipe yourself." Rising from the bed, off balance, I almost run to my parents' room, but I remember my dad doesn't like to be disturbed when he's sleeping. But I want my dad; I need someone to challenge the bogeyman for holding me in bondage . . . something very wrong has happened where trust is badly skewed, but I didn't know what or how to define it.

I pulled up my undershorts and stood in the bathroom for a very long time. For some reason I look in the mirror . . . it was the first time I saw shame and abandonment . . . not knowing what I felt . . . only perhaps a fierce emotion I'd never understand . . . It seemed I could not blink, but I could be alone to hate . . . I reached up and cut the light off.

I don't know how long I stayed there, but I never locked the door . . . perhaps I only locked people out of my life, out of my space . . . perhaps I demolished my chance of a truer survival; after all, wasn't it my fault because I didn't cry . . . I didn't scream . . . I never did.

In travels throughout my young life, sex education from the streets, school, magazines under my father's bed, the childish childhood whispers . . . all told me, my cousin had done something very, very wrong. He set in motion a humiliating descent into my own battle of addictions: tools to run from and extol such a devastating catastrophe. Thus began a sad serenade of hate . . . (that would later let me hate my brother).

Thus began a sad serenade of hate

R. L. LOVE

Another Side

On Mother's Day
On Father's Day
I thought of love so true
I bought a card
I wrote a poem
And gifts for both of you

A pocket watch
A new TV
Even flowers too
A leather belt
A brand-new iron
Just for the two of you

But when doors closed . . . there was a part
. . . the world could never see
there was another side . . . no one would hear my plea

*I still wonder why /
I tell sweet lies
so true*

No one would ever know
No one could ever tell
The pain I held in me
No one felt that belt
Or that ironing cord
Or lies from that TV

and still . . . on Mother's Day I write
on Father's Day I smile
And think of each of you
I still wonder how
I still wonder why
I tell sweet lies so true

DARNELL FORD

Christmas

This is the season to be jolly, the time of year when everything is supposed to come together and when you surround yourself with those who love you. This is the time of year when love and harmony and peace fills the polluted air. From turkey feast to *me cumple años el cinco de enero*, everything is supposed to be fun, things are supposed to make sense, and everybody's supposed to love everybody.

*Whenever my family
comes together for
whatever the reason
it's like a royal
rumble. It's a flat-
out free-for-all.*

Whoever made these rules sure as hell didn't give them to my family. I don't even think my family has a traditional set of rules for coming together. But they sure as hell need one—a set of rules, that is. Whenever my family comes together for whatever the reason it's like a royal rumble. It's a flat-out free-for-all. Every man for himself. Instead of using the holidays as a time of warmth and love, they create this forum for bringing all their issues toward each other. Causing all hell to break loose. Usually after the smoke clears we begin to rebuild our relationships, but that's not always a guarantee.

I've got two of the greatest grandparents in the world. Together they're the sweetest couple you've ever seen. They ain't the sweetest people, but they keep it real. They're there when you need 'em, but they curse you out if you're wrong. My grandparents have no problem telling it to you like it is. And no problem throwing your ass out on the streets. Their house is usually where the family comes together during the holidays. They have eight kids—four boys and four girls.

My mom, the oldest of all their kids, is pretty straightforward too. She never had a problem kicking her brothers and sister in the ass. I guess that's why she's never had a problem with kicking me in the ass either. I've got two brothers and two sisters. Mom is, however, the most spiritual person in our family and the sole reason for my faith and spirituality. Whenever a fight breaks out or someone's feeling bad or something terrible happens, it's usually my mom who brings the family together in prayer.

One of my mom's sisters is totally opposite her. Looks are very deceiving. My aunt Key is this really mean, bitchy, and aggressive woman. You would never be able to tell by simply looking at her because she's very attractive and appears to be very sophisticated and ladylike. But let me remind you, looks are very deceiving.

My aunt Key is a Chicago police officer who patrols the rough streets of the west side of Chicago. You've got to be tough to do that and she's been on the force for ten years now. She used to be married to this real cool dude who played basketball for Chicago State. But she ended up beating his ass, throwing him out on the streets and divorcing him after she caught him cheating. One thing I love about my aunt Key is the exciting stories she tells about her job and the things she sees on a daily basis. I remember when she told us about this dude she shot up because he was shooting at her. That really made me look at her and police officers in a different way.

Now I've got two other aunts, Deb and Dee. These names are short for Debra and Darlene. They're both very sensitive and intelligent. We usually only see Deb and Dee around this time of year because they're always at school. Now that both of their kids are grown, they've become professional students. Because they're in school they really act like they know everything about everything and everybody. When these two get together, the gossip is on. If you've got some secret business, they all in it. They ain't got no shame in exploiting you. They're always talking, mostly about my uncles because my uncles' issues really are true classics. But their favorite subject is the youngest of my grandparents kids, my uncle Mike.

Uncle Mike is what my cousins and I call him. Big Mike is what everybody else calls him. You see, he's not that big actually, but his reputation is very big. On the surface he's a really friendly guy, but my aunts criticize him because he's a big drug dealer and highly respected on Chicago's South Side. Deb and Dee talk about Mike like a dog. They say he's doing the devil's work and he ain't no good, but whenever it's time to pass out gifts they the main ones with their hands out. They start off downing the man but they finish by praising him for giving them some expensive perfume or some brand-name clothes.

Today my uncle Wayne is minister at the Christ Baptist Church in Chicago. Five years ago he was the meanest, toughest pimp I ever knew.

Uncle Mike has always been generous with his money. He's given some of the greatest gifts ever, like gold watches, diamonds, and cash out of his pocket. I like when he forgets about you because he ends up feeling guilty and pays you a large sum of money in order to compensate for his guilty feeling. One year, he forgot about me and dished out five twenty-dollar bills. I felt like I was ballin' then, flashing my money like my name was Uncle Mike. All in all, what Uncle Mike does is not right, but he's a great guy with a beautiful heart who knows who he is. I only wish my uncle Wayne knew who he was.

Today my uncle Wayne is minister at the Christ Baptist Church in Chicago. Five years ago he was the meanest, toughest pimp I ever knew. When he talked, he stomped his feet and flashed his hands. You would have to give him your undivided attention when he spoke, or else you would miss something, because the man talked so fast and everything he said he had a metaphor for.

It was funny, some of the things he used to do, like he used to have a problem with respecting women, every female, including his sisters, belonged on the "ho stroll" making somebody some money. He would say to his sisters, you need to get your ass out my face and on down to the track. That's when all hell would break loose. My grandma would usually end up kicking him out her house.

Those were the good old days. Today he's in the business of saving souls. He's not working on the stroll anymore but in the pulpit. However, sometimes he gets a little overexcited and a little old behavior presents itself in the middle of giving his sermon. I fall out laughing when I see him stomping his feet and flashing his hands. My uncle Wayne is a character, a very hilarious character. He's got six kids by four mommas, four girls and two boys. Uncle Wayne had a problem with being faithful to one woman back in the day but I think he's happy with the woman he's with now, which at least I can say about him and not my Uncle Paul.

Uncle Paul just can't seem to find a woman who's right for him. He's the most faithful guy on the planet. I don't think he could cheat if he wanted to. But for the strangest reason he's always ending up with the sleaziest women in Chicago. Like this chick he's with now. The biggest slut in the Midwest. I don't know where he found her. Probably on Uncle Wayne's ho stroll. They been together ever since Paul was released from prison. It just never seems to fit right. Here you have this big, muscular, handsome mechanic who only wants a woman that will love him for being who he is and here you have this slim, sleazy, slutty woman who is willing to spread her legs for anybody at any time. It's just not registering with me. Paul is either blind or the most naive man I've ever known. They always fighting about where she's been and what happened to the money he gave her and why the car ain't got no gas in it. Uncle Paul is hard-headed too, because the whole family tells him over and over to leave this broad alone but he just doesn't want to listen. He would rather just go get a fifth of Martel and drink 'til his misery is gone.

I've got one more uncle. Uncle Fitz, short for Fitzgerald, who is currently in prison for bank robbery.

KRISTIAN MARINE

My Secret

It's an ugly whisper inside me that I've heard since I could remember

It's an ugly whisper inside me that I've heard since I could
    remember
I believe that it has a foundation in events that happened
Before I could remember anything
There are so many possible reasons why I was put up for
    adoption
So many reasons why my parents kept my siblings and not me

Among these many reasons are very good ones, very responsible
    ones
But that's not something the heart of an infant can discern
The heart of that infant now adult still doesn't know exactly
Why I was given up

If I could be given up by my very own mother, / What's to stop anyone else from giving me up?

Wasn't I worth the time, the effort, the sacrifice to keep and
    love?
If I could be given up by my very own mother,
What's to stop anyone else from giving me up?
That's my secret

Since I couldn't convince my own mother to keep me
Anyone who might adopt me must be a great soul, right,
To love that unloved, unlovable child?
So I'd better be a good kid so I don't lose their love too, right?

And all along the voice whispering says they couldn't possibly
    love me
I've got them fooled so I better not slip up

They try and try to love you but how could they?
You were bad from the beginning
You weren't good enough for your own parents
But maybe, maybe they'll give you another chance

So I ask for another chance and, if granted,
I can't believe my good fortune
And more ahead to earn their love back
Since I never really had it in the first place

I am tempted to believe sometimes
But if I believe I have it, I know it's only temporary
Or because they don't yet understand me
And then I go about the business, the only business I know for
    sure
That I'm good at

Proving the whispers right, of ruining relationships, of losing
    love
Love that I never really had, or at least never deserved

All I can remember are relationships that end in separation
After a period of attachment,
And some level of thirst. That is a generalization of course,
But some days that is the truth I live in.

WESLEY SIMMS

Why Me, Mama?

I'm thinking about the day you slapped me and sent me to my
room.
A stick, belt, switch, extension cord, hairbrush, hand, fist, and
also a broom.
These are just a few of the things you used to break my spirit.
You used to whip me and beat me where the whole
neighborhood could hear it.

Eight years old, Ma, what could I possibly do to deserve such
abuse and pain?
All the words of hate you screamed still remain on my brain.
My life has been scarred, filled with doubt, worry, and trauma.
I haven't seen you in two decades, yet still have compassion
for you, Mama.

How could you bring me into this world and then hate me at a
tender age?
I'm not my father, Mama, but became the recipient of all your
rage.
My wounds healed, but your words are forever etched in my
heart.
I was only a kid, Mama, when my life began to fall apart.

For those who feel my shame, these words touch and heal.
Those cards was dealt to a kid, but now I'm old enough to deal.

*For those who feel
my shame, these
words touch and
heal. / Those cards
was dealt to a kid,
but now I'm old
enough to deal.*

WESLEY SIMMS

Untitled

My mother locked me in a closet for about nine to twelve hours and told me if I came out she'd beat my ass until I wished I was dead. I remember her hitting me with a two-by-four and dislocating my shoulder, I went to the hospital, and not once did my mom say sorry or show compassion . . . Yet all the beatings I endured physically were nothing to words like *worthless, sorry ass, no-good-for-nothing nigga, ignorant mothafucka, bring your stupid ass in this house, I can't stand the sight of you, get the fuck out of my damn face* . . . My mom has never held me and said, It'll be okay, baby, or, Wesley I love you and always will love you . . . I can't be sure, but as long as I can remember, I don't remember ever being hugged. I don't ever remember my mom giving me words of encouragement. I remember my mom came to school and beat my ass in the hallway with a belt buckle, it seemed the whole school saw me get that beating . . . My mom whipped me simply because I was born by the man who made my family's life a living hell.

I think back to all the names my mom called me as she beat me with an extension cord, leaving welts from my shoulders to my ankles while she screamed I wouldn't amount to shit or she's going to kill my stupid ass or whatever she would holler as I got beating after beating. I guess she was right 'cause somewhere around those beatings I chose to not care. I started to believe I'd amount to zero. I never had new clothes. Everything I ever owned as a child was hand-me-down. On family day at school my parents never was there 'cause I would never tell them 'cause I didn't want them to be drunk at my school.

Before my father moved in, my mom would bring different men home and close her bedroom door. He'd always be gone when we woke up the next morning. Once my father moved in he would beat my mom real bad. I can say our house woke up plenty nights hearing my mom getting beat viciously. There have been times he broke my mom's arm, broke her jaw, sent her to the hospital with

*Today I'm a
reflection of my
childhood.*

cracked ribs. Another time he split my mom's eye wide open. My sister says she was sexually assaulted by my father. I remember my brother saw my father kick my mom in her stomach and my brother hit my father in the head with a wrench. Later that night my mother whipped my brother for helping her. My father used to sock my brothers in the face with his fist or kick them like he would kick a ball . . . I can't remember one single day that my father was not drunk—ever! I can't remember one day!

I never told anyone what took place in my household. Before anyone judges me, please remember, I'm the youngest of four kids and I was not even eight years of age so I didn't know how to deal with these issues. Today I'm a reflection of my childhood. I'm just now speaking on it. I used to make up perfect family stories and fantasies about my family of love and closeness because I'm ashamed of who I am, I'm ashamed of who I've become. My life has been buried in shame, buried in secrets. I would never tell anyone that I suffered at the hands of my biological mother, things like my father sexually abused my sister.

My mother is still living and even to this day she doesn't care for me. Can I overcome this pain?

I need to stop right here 'cause it hurts so much. I'm sorry but I can't continue right now.

MARGO PERIN

Och, Aye

On our way from the airport to Ayr, in Scotland, where we were to spend our vacation, the taxi driver stopped the car at the top of a hill and told us to look below. "Och, isn't it bonny?" he said, and even though I didn't know what he was saying, I knew he meant for us to admire his country. I squinted down at the gray dampness and thought how ugly it was. The sky was so low it ran into the stark hills of the Scottish lowlands. At my feet were rows of stone houses and rain-streaked roads. Purple sprigs of heather provided the only relief from the unremitting dreariness.

"That's our national flower," said the driver.

"Can we go now?" I asked, shuddering with cold.

The driver laughed. "Ay, wee lassie, you'll nae be lang hame."

"What?"

I flinched as he chucked me under the chin. "You'll know soon enough."

On the airplane over the whirring of the engines, I had overheard my mother tell my brother that we were going to a place called Butlins Holiday Camp.

"What's a holiday camp?" Lance had yawned.

"It's a place where families stay on vacation." My mother's voice sounded compressed, high, like a balloon. "They have a swimming pool and lots of activities. It's all organized."

"Why do we need people to organize us?" I asked, leaning across the aisle.

"Don't start that again," she answered crossly.

"Is there a roller coaster?" asked Max, who was sitting behind her.

My mother opened her compact and pressed her lips together. "I don't know," she said plaintively. "Stop bothering me."

Butlins turned out to be the exact opposite of what I'd imagined. It was built like a small town, its streets dividing chalets in neat lines, like a prison camp. Loudspeakers were placed strategically throughout the area and every morning a bugle would go off, followed by a gleeful "Good Morning, Campers," our signal that sleep was now out of the question. Struggling out of bed in the cold damp of the small, one-room cottages, I stuffed my body into jeans and headed with the crowds towards the mess hall, large enough for tanks and riot police if we stepped out of line. We stood in line clutching tin trays with the other vacation refugees and were doled

Purple sprigs of heather provided the only relief from the unremitting dreariness.

*we found some
cans of beer behind
the mess hall and
got so drunk we
stopped caring.*

out rubbery scrambled eggs and greasy little sausages, cornflakes, and tea in chipped china cups. My parents seemed to forget about their no-sugar rule and didn't say anything as I heaped giant handfuls onto everything.

One half hour was allowed by the camp rules for breakfast, enough time to get into a fight to distract ourselves from how depressing everything was. Then we were off to group activities, swimming, calisthenics, bingo, or sing-alongs. Elizabeth and I wove between the chalets, stealing chocolate from the candy store and smoking cigarettes. We couldn't understand what anyone was saying. But we found some cans of beer behind the mess hall and got so drunk we stopped caring. Then we got hold of a tube of glue and tried to get high in the bathroom, a row of concrete stalls, cold and gloomy. Maybe we weren't holding the paper bag right, but after rolling around for a few minutes pretending to be stoned, we gave up and went back to our weaving.

The people at the camp had cheeks rubbed raw by the wind, watery, red-rimmed eyes, sandy hair that was singularly straight and stringy, and short, stubby noses. They all spoke English, however unintelligible, giving the impression we had something in common. But it was an illusion and, to them, I must have seemed as foreign as they were to me. It was like none of us knew where to place each other. The air was laced with an iciness blown in fresh from the Atlantic, but the people wore bathing suits because it was summer. No doubt on June 21, the loudspeakers had blared an order for everyone to remove their clothes. My mother came back from town one day with a heap of sweaters, red and yellow lines crisscrossing them, good for target practice when we all had had enough of each other, cooped up inside because it was too fucking freezing to open the door. That's what Ava kept saying, "If you don't get out of my fucking way I'm going to fucking kill you. Now shut that fucking door. It's fucking freezing."

It was the worst for Ava. She was sixteen. She had her whole life in New York, friends, a boyfriend, high school. It was better she was saying *fucking* all the time, rather than doing damage to herself or one of us.

A beefy orange-haired man who was also on vacation introduced himself with a smirk as Rabbie Burns—like we were supposed to know what *that* meant—and offered to take us into town in a taxi. He got in the back next to me and Elizabeth and put his arm around me so that his hand was cupping my breast. I pressed my arm tightly against my side to make him move it but he only squeezed harder. When we got back to our cottage I sat on the windowsill and cried. He'd made me feel dirty and ugly, like there was something crawling in my underwear. When Elizabeth was called away by my mother, I fished under the bed for the glue and went off to the bathroom. This time my head got a little fuzzy and I fell on the toilet shaking and giggling. But after a while all I felt was dizzy and sick so I flushed it down, watching the tube spin in the gray water. I slammed the bathroom door on the way out, turned back, and slammed it again. I couldn't wait to get back home.

As my parents promised, we did stay at Butlins for three weeks, and I counted off the days on my fingers. When it was time to leave, my father took us for a drive down narrow roads hugging the rain-spattered hills. Bulbous black clouds refusing to either burst open with rain or clear off hung dismally in the sky as we bumped along into a small town and veered into a street lined with houses squatting behind small stone walls. After pulling into a driveway my father said, "Get out of the car and help Mom unpack."

There was the longest, whitest pause. Everything stopped. My breathing, the sound of rain hitting the roof of the car, my mother tapping her nails on the dashboard. There was something ringing in my ears, and I felt like I'd been hit so hard on the head my eyes had jammed.

A scrambling noise broke through the ringing. Ava was jumping out of the car. "I knew it!" From a distance I heard her bursting into

It was better she was saying fucking *all the time, rather than doing damage to herself or one of us.*

*stuffed with
somebody else's
furniture and
somebody
else's story.*

tears. Over to my left I could see that Elizabeth was paralyzed; her eyes were fixed on the dreary-looking house, her jaw rigid.

My father was blinking at something in the distance; I became aware of the smell of him filling up the car. "You know as well as I do how bad things have been getting in the States." He was waving his arms in the air. I knew enough to dodge out of the way, even though I was fused to the seat. "The schools—" he gestured towards Ava, who was weeping into a tree in the front yard. "The Vietnam War—" he nodded at my brothers, pale and frozen in the back of the car.

I don't remember what happened next, how I managed to lift my legs from the floor and unstick myself from the seat and make my way into our new home that was stuffed with somebody else's furniture and somebody else's story.

Helensburgh. Old, cold, grimy, our ground control from the UFO, where life was supposed to continue as if we had always lived here, no questions asked, even though my father had changed the spelling of our name, from Perin with one *r* to Perrin with two. French, distinguished, but not very smart if anyone was looking hard enough for us.

There it was all of a sudden, P-e-r-r-i-n, on my mother's lips when she spelled it out for anyone on the phone, on bills that arrived at the house, on name tags she sewed into our ugly new navy-blue gym clothes in which we were forced to dance the Scottish jig like it meant something, on our school reports. *Perrin,* from a long line of French Hugenots as my father subtly suggested over his newspaper one day, and also kind of English, like Lea and Perrins sauce.

The change was seamless, with no discussion. And just as seamlessly I and all of my siblings adopted our new name like we had been called that our entire lives, without demanding an explanation or uttering a word of protest. We answered to it without flinching, handing in school essays with it emblazoned at the top, later filling out National Health Insurance forms with it, job applications, and even later our own passports. We never talked about it, not even to each other. We knew by instinct and experience that this was how things were to be from now on. But underneath it all, even though it was only the change of one letter, my new name made me feel confused and even more disconnected. I had taken my name for granted, it was something I didn't have to question, and now it was gone. One more building block of who I was had vanished into thin air.

At supper in the pine-paneled kitchen that first night, Max held up his fork. "Hey, this says Butlins on it."

"So does mine," said Tristam. His hair fell over his forehead in uneven tufts.

My mother shrugged and gave a small, mischievous laugh. "We couldn't move into a house with nothing, now, could we?"

Thus began our *carte blanche* to steal from restaurants. The boys would grab the curls of butter at the center of the table and wolf them down, then one or another of them would slip the butter dish into his pocket, boasting later how many he'd gotten. After grabbing large handfuls of sugar cubes, I took forks and knives, the shinier the better, and Elizabeth glasses and silver spoons. Our stealing rose to a frenzy so that by the time my father took us to a fancy restaurant a few years later, the entire set of ceramic goblets and plates on our table was missing when we left. Elizabeth and I spent half the dinner rushing to the restroom to add to our collection, which we stored at the top of one of the cisterns, giggling hysterically as we gasped down our cigarettes.

My parents themselves seemed to be past their stealing phase, at least of the restaurant kind, and they and everyone else at the restaurant, waitresses, diners and the *maitre d'*, were either blind or too drunk to see our waddling out with our booty in our underwear, pants, and purses. We took other people's belongings in place of belonging, and stole as much as we could.

We took other people's belongings in place of belonging, and stole as much as we could.

Education

Mom tells me to stop fooling around and get in there with my friends from kindergarten. How can she call them my friends? I've only been in school for one week. She doesn't know that they're all watching me hoping I'll crash and burn, like I did with my ABCs, everyone laughing at me, the noise almost did me in.

—Ernest Fisher

PATRICIA ROBINSON

Untitled

When I was in high school I became a teacher's assistant for a woman English teacher by the name of Una Keenan. She gave me a ride to school every day and knowing her made a very big difference in my life. She was a graduate and one of her favorites was a classic black story, *Jubilee*. Her favorite poem was called "If."

Besides having a work and study program at the JFK school, I also did some ironing at her home for extra money. Her husband was a U.S. postal worker. I also had another part-time job at the post office at night after school. The Keenans made so much possible for all the youth in our neighborhood, especially when it comes to the old-fashioned southern work ethics.

My foster parents also worked hard every day. My foster dad, Mr. Roosevelt Latimore, worked at first for Thompson Products as a cook, as I was told, and later as a brick cement mason and finally as president of a company union. He was then a major maintenance person. He encouraged other people to become foster parents and there were many people who worked for TWR in our neighborhood.

He really believed in education as the answer to a person's problem. He only had a sixth-grade education. He had been born in Rome, Georgia, and raised in Alabama. He had fourteen or fifteen brothers and sisters. He was a triplet, triplets and up run in all our families. My foster mother, Mrs. Birdie Marie Latimore, married at thirteen. She had already finished high school. A few blocks away lived Reverend and Mrs. Julian Camp. He was a Baptist minister and his wife Charity was my foster mother's older sister.

🔲

R. L. LOVE

The Rope

A few days prior, some friends and I would sneak behind the elementary school we attended. The wet silky grass became our own African safari as we uprooted old boards and rocks to discover another world. Small green and yellow snakes were the most dangerous reptiles in the world and salamanders were old ancient dinosaurs. Our inquisitiveness would lead us to discover smooth baseball-size rocks which were used to form the old goldfish pond. We touched the unusual smoothness as we tossed them like Babe and Willie . . . one hits the rear wall—we look up from the sound—windows! Rocks began to fly and windows burst into rainbow splinters; and the alarm's shrill sound says it's time to run.

Monday morning blues had Momma and me in audience with the principal. I only felt a hostile, robust tone which effectively determined I would never appear inside the dismal doors of that particular school. Walking through the gates for the last time, I heard my mother say, "Wait 'til I tell your father." My only hope became: Where is God? I guess busy with the angels . . . I never felt so abandoned.

Later that day in a silent enraged voice he summoned, "Go downstairs." Finally together; almost an embrace, for finally I was getting his attention . . . I knew my stomach fluttered that lie, but still, walking down the stairs I knew . . . and I also knew I would not cry.

The garage never seemed so creepy until I saw the rope, and then it became a hopeless cavern of despair.

"Stand right there and take off your shirt . . . I spend money to make sure you get the education I never had, and you waste it!" Wordlessly my shirt fluttered to the floor . . . I felt betrayed and it wasn't my favorite shirt anymore.

Rough bounds of rope began to secure my tense body to an insensitive vertical support beam. The gallant spirit to not cry stayed with me, even though I knew it was time to die . . . the first wicked sharp blow would stun me to my toes as I struggled to breathe and not scream. The second blow was so fierce across my shoulders, I could smell rope dust and blood mingle in the air like a cold strange blast in a barren dry place—so that was where my despondent soul would run. Still, I felt its punctual rhythm . . . I even see the rope coming; hypnotized—it's snaking through the air like an old rusty whip that could not hurt as it caresses my neck and the beam slaps me in the face. Somehow I discarded myself as each furious, biting strike tore into my back—I would not cry. I lost count in this savage and violent death: my childhood died, and any desire for education was destroyed; all buried under tears that mixed with blood on a cold, repulsive concrete grave. I never felt the freedom, only . . . "Go clean yourself up." I stood in darkness and knew, I am not a child . . . only baptized in the ashes of someone's rage . . .

I stood in darkness and knew, I am not a child . . . only baptized in the ashes of someone's rage

🔳

GREG CARTER

Mickey Pleads the Fifth

The old Crockett swimming pool, I think it was 1966.
I was this golden human boy shackled under the looming gaze
Of the deities of Beechwood Ave.

Samson and Delilah
Fred and Wilma
Phyllis and Fang
Mrs. Carter

Poolside 1966, the hi-fi wired to the speaker horns,
The child, his known world eclipsed by the music, is pinned
   down
But I wish I could say, "Duo Dina" or Oscar Peterson.
It was not to be, I was assassinated by "My Baby Does the
   Hanky-Panky."
All I could see was some well-fed hairy chicks doing the jerk
And a bunch of dudes looking like Jesus, not all of whom could
   swim, some tried to walk
And were now in various stages of drowning.
Lifeguard dove to the rescue in three feet of water and may never
   walk.
The bottom of the pool was getting crowded,
I now knew what the lady on the roof of Playland was laughing
   at,
She was laughing at fate.

The seeds of rebellion were sown.

Were you ever at the 7-Eleven across from my grammar school?
Where school began at 2:45, my teachers were not laureates,
   they loitered.
Shoot, I thought, when you got older you just hung out in
   parking lots and gave lectures.
I was transfixed, already applicable, become unerring.
Graduation was held a coupla hundred times a year.
When they bit my mind my ideas were the shape of them teeth,
And because my notes are written in scar, I am able to remember
   a particular professor.

We called him Mickey Pleads the Fifth, no one knew his story,
    he was there sometimes like a crow.
No finely aged attaché case for Mickey, 'twas Rainier ale
    wrapped in a pint bag as is proper.

7:00 AM the asphalt is already shimmering with dreams lost the
    night before.
Georgia St. 1971 and Mickey has on a pair of Chevron coveralls,
    Chuck Taylors and a fedora.
His eyes are extinct. When he leveled them things at you, you
    could not move.
The words "Hey kid" fueled by creaky lungs still raise the
    hackles on my neck.
You see, to lay eyes on this caricature was to be hypnotized.
We did not stand a chance, we would not be home for dinner.
Fact is, Mickey was teaching us to raise our chins and accept the
    degradation with panache.

Teachers got old and died, masking the horrors of a world that
    would chew us up anyway.
Mickey saw it, he saw to it that we'd grow tongues that forked,
    in order to seethe.
If I could see him now I don't know if I would hurt him, or shake
    his hand.

I'm a journeyman myself now, adequately tainted.
Was cause for many uneaten plates at the table,
Until one day, I ran the fever of wisdom that shook me into
    knowing
That I gotta go back to those heady days
And change the very first professed mindset I ever had.

*This was
my mom's way
of telling me how
important school is.*

TIMOTHY HECK

Education

I got suspended from school for a couple of days. I was met by an unsurprising dose of mental and physical violence. This was my mom's way of telling me how important school is. To show me that she wasn't playing either, she took all my new clothes, tossed them into the backyard, soaked them with a bottle of lighter fluid, and set them ablaze.

Home

I had no home but my car.

—Kristian Marine

▣

MICHAEL FRANCIS

Welcome Home

I remember, as it is in the nature of such memories, with softer edges, blurred surroundings, and echoing sounds, a memory of the feelings I had as I hopped down from the transport van. I remember the sweet smells of salt water and fresh-cut damp grass and a warm sun upon my face. I remember the feeling of comfort as well as a feeling of apprehension of new territories as I looked overhead, shuffling my chained feet closer to those steps up to the grill gate of the main entrance of San Quentin, California.

I can never forget that sick feeling of belonging, of coming home, of inner peace.

I remember the belly chain tight on my stomach, fists clenched, footsteps mentally measured as to not overextend the reach of the length of the chain between my ankles and the length of the chain that returned to my belly. We used to be able to tell a 'first termer' by the way he walked in full chains and leg shackles. I remember as we were taken through the main courtyard, passed A/C, the CO yelling out like some sick opera singer, "Escort," almost like a yodel or something. Guess you'd have had to have been there.

I remember seeing all the homeboys I had heard were dead nodding or waving to me as we walked down the ramp, passed the old hole, now the "Gooner" office, down through the lower yard to R&R for processing, where I was met by yet more familiar faces and a first cigarette in ninety days as my Indian "Iron House Family" greeted me and started the old tradition of clowning me for coming back yet again.

Yes, I was home again. The inscription may say "Abandon hope, all ye who enter," but it translated to me as "Welcome home."

The inscription may say "Abandon hope, all ye who enter," but it translated to me as "Welcome home."

R. L. LOVE

Looking for a Home

One time, as a boy, I ran away from home
No further than upstairs . . . but that empty unit made
the place of peace to me . . . and silence I would save

Since then I've often wondered where home is
                                where home was
                                  or where home can be

And of course I've heard . . . home is where you find it
                              home is where you make it
                              home is where your heart is
Well . . .

An abandoned car . . . an empty house . . . allies and doorways
Yes these places said
Home is where I found it

A jail cell . . . a brother's couch . . . a friend's hidden room
Yes these places gave
Home is where I made it

My sister's home . . . an ex-wife's bed . . . an old mobile home
Yes these places whispered
Home is where my heart is

Yet . . . in forty-eight years of life . . . I still can't sing that song
You know the one they sing . . . "Home Sweet Home"
And maybe it's not the home . . . but silence I seek within
Maybe I search for peace . . . so I can live again

*Since then I've often
wondered where
home is / where
home was / or where
home can be*

R. L. LOVE

No Thank You

Homeless
Homeless
Homeless again
The unforgivable sin

And the pennies I would save
Labor Ready gave
Pennies that I count
That never seem to mount

Then she came along
Singing a needed song
Come to my home
We need not be alone

Later to my surprise
Her temper would somehow rise
Did you do this—did you do that
Have you seen my purple hat

So after a short while
I lost my only smile
I couldn't take it anymore
As I walked out the door

Homeless
Homeless
Homeless again

*Homeless again / I
welcome / I welcome
/ This unforgivable
sin*

I welcome
I welcome
This unforgivable sin

MARGO PERIN

Mexico

One hot August night when I was seven, I was lying asleep in bed in the shadow of the blue and red Pepsi-Cola sign blinking across New York's East River. The next minute, I was squeezed between my siblings in the backseat of a dusty cab, staring out in confusion at a sunrise of burnt orange mud and brick buildings. My father's hair was shimmering black in the sun when the driver let him out to stretch his legs at the top of a downwardly spiraling town.

"Where are we?" asked my brother.

"On vacation," my father said vacantly as he lit a cigarette.

We pulled up to a house the color of a dusky sunset that my father called a *hacienda*, the word floating off his tongue like rain. There was purple everywhere, bougainvillea, on the walls, along the bushes, branching up to the sky. No one said we were moving, but soon every morning a school bus belching black smoke turned up to take us to our new school, and apparently everything was to go on as normal: breakfast, lunch, supper, no talking back, bed when my parents ordered, Sunday outings.

Behind the adobe walls of our house in Mexico where nobody knew us, we were to live secluded inside my parents' swift and silent recreation of a universe that no amount of questions could penetrate. We would be sealed in by a membrane of lies so thick, my parents themselves would seem to believe what they had fabricated. My father was a bona fide businessman. We were here

*I didn't know
that already any
pretense of safety
and belonging
had ended, that
we would never be
going home, that
there never again
would be "home."*

on vacation. I didn't know that already any pretense of safety and belonging had ended, that we would never be going home, that there never again would be "home."

One glistening, dewy Sunday, after we had lived in Cuernavaca for several months, my father took us to an opera matinee in Mexico City. My sisters and brothers and I were dressed up in matching tartan outfits, shorts for the boys, skirts for the girls, with white shirts and jackets. My father seemed happy, his face was flushed and grinning, and my mother was drifting in a cloud of perfume with a dreamy expression.

In the intermission we filed into the plush velvet bar and my father was just about to go off to get something to drink when a woman in a red dress waylaid him halfway down the wide passageway. Everything on her was red; she had red cheeks and red painted nails and pointy red stilettos, even a shiny red purse, and she greeted him as if she were excited and pleased to see him. Her hand was on his arm, her face was broad cheeked, and she had a tiny brown beauty mark near her lips. My mother stood by my father's side smiling tightly and I watched while they chatted back and forth. The woman's voice was loud and boisterous, grainy like a million beads of sand were coating her throat. "Arden, what are you doing here? What a surprise! Are you here on vacation?"

My father spoke in a quiet murmur, looking friendly and relaxed. When she'd gone, his face turned dark with anger at being discovered. My mother stiffened and muttered, "Why don't people mind their own business?" I didn't know what she meant; the woman had looked so happy to see them, especially my father, whose hands were slightly trembling.

I stood on tiptoes and tugged my father's jacket sleeve. "Who was that, Dad?"

My father froze. Then he grinned down at me, his freshly laundered handkerchief a perfect white triangle in his breast pocket. "Why, that's Mrs. Whosiwhatsi," he said magnanimously.

I broke into a giggle. "Mrs. Whosiwhatsi," I repeated as I stood in the plush lobby of a beautiful theater, in this country that was as glamorous as my father. How lovely was the ravishing color and heat of Mexico; how sweet the seduction of my father, the suggestion that there was a heart underneath, and a place called home. In that moment, the radiance and beauty of geography and biology, of home and safety, flowed seamlessly into one other. But at the same time, a sliver of darkness broke through my father's illuminated image: I suddenly understood that we were in hiding, and that it was dangerous.

When we arrived home, our thick wooden front door was half-way open. "What—?" exclaimed my father, and ran into the house with my mother close behind. Through the doorway, I could see the sheets and blankets of my couch-bed in the living room had been torn off, and my pillow hurled onto the tiled floor.

"Arden—" my mother cried, her eyes wide in alarm, as my father dashed into their bedroom. Clothes and papers and dresser drawers were strewn all over the floor. The mattress was in shreds, pillows slashed, the white lace bedspread heaped in the corner, covered in feathers. Books had been thrown viciously against the wall, the threads of their thick hemp binding blasted through.

"What were they looking for?" my mother moaned, crouching on her knees over her broken, but still full, jewelry box. My father was ransacking through a stack of papers, searching for what might be missing. He looked frantic. "What are you doing here?" he snapped as he suddenly threw open the door and caught me spying on them.

"Nothing," I spluttered.

He pushed me out of the way. "Tell everyone to get ready."

His fingers shook as he made circles in the telephone dial. *"Non, el primero! Taxi. Si!"* he was shouting as I ran outside.

There was a frenzy of packing, and then the dream of Mexico was gone.

I suddenly understood that we were in hiding, and that it was dangerous.

Love

*Deep down inside I wonder why I've never been loved
the way I want to be loved.*

—Stephen Logan

AJA CAYETANO WITH DALE WALTON

Untitled

Skin
Butter pecan latte cappiocha
With a scent of man (cinnamon) twist.
I begin
You begin
Your serenade
Like a renegade Zorro
You announce in every language and alphabet
"Birds my girl"
"Birds my girl"
But, but where's Bird? . . .
Locked in a cage where she can't be freed
And you, on the streets still wanting. Me!

KIMBERLEY WRIGHT

Untitled

I learned to love someone unconditionally
Not for who they are or what they done
I don't have to pretend or claim top gun
I didn't appreciate her at first for one reason or another
Because she shows me it ain't about being the best lover

*Moments like this
is what I share /
With the lady of my
dreams, oh my, you
can't compare*

We cry
We talk
We laugh
We fight
Then we go to church and praise God with all our might
Moments like this is what I share
With the lady of my dreams, oh my, you can't compare
(Appreciate people, places, things, before it's too late.)

JANICE ARMSTRONG

Love

It's been a long time since I've felt the way I feel about a man I
sleep this man I eat this man I walk this man I dream this man I
pray about this I even try to forget about this but deep down inside
I feel something pulling and tugging at my heart and it causes me
to be off balance.

BRIAN BAIRD

Anathema

I hate to love, I hate to hate
Is San Francisco a city or state?
A state of mind is what you'll find
An anathema to all mankind

Jogging my memory
Heightening my senses

I once was a dope fiend
Flipping the dopamine

An anathema is what I see
Looking at something that used to be me
I used to look rugged and all tore up
It makes me want to go and throw up

All of the memories flooding me now
Showing me who, where, what, why, and how!
My eyes go blind as I start to find
I used to be mean, now I am kind

Opposites attract, like Ozzy and Reba
This is my story of my anathema
Tenderloin homeless crack addicts abound
Shots being fired, can't you hear the sound

It hurts my ears and I start to fear
I can't believe that I actually live here
Both of my marriages fell all to shit
Some days I want to scream, "Give me a hit!"

Now I'm in love with a wonderful guy
Being in here makes me want to cry
I miss him so, I want to go
I hope I don't end up back on skid row

Seeing the things that I love to hate
Maybe I'll move somewhere out of state
Away from the anathema of my life
I'll even take my husband, and leave behind the wife

RON SALKIN

Kim

Quite often, I have written about my late wife Kim, the woman who was my entire life, my best friend, and the person whom I thought I would spend the rest of my life with, until that fateful Friday night in November of '93 when she was suddenly taken from me. We had pretty much always led a life of responsibility, paying bills, going to work every day, having lots of fun whether it was at home or out on the town.

When I first met Kim it was quite a painful experience for me for two reasons, first because she came over to my apartment as my roommate Rick's friend. He had just met her and was trying his best Steve Suave/Sam Smooth moves on her. Second, when I first saw her they were outside our place and she was helping Rick clean out his car. I was on my way to the store. I walked out of the front door of my apartment, and saw her staring and smiling at me. I turned around to see who she was smiling at, because I didn't think I was fortunate enough to have a beautiful hottie like that checking me out as intensely as she was. When I realized that it was me that she was smiling at, I promptly smiled back at her, turned back around to continue my trip to the store and walked smack dab into a telephone pole face first. My ears were first, then my face as both got hotter than the surface of the sun in August, from embarrassment. She laughed, and I tried playing it off like I meant to do that but that didn't fly as I continued walking to the store with the now self-appointed title "King Doofus of the World." I thought, Great! How the hell am I going to ask her out now, not even knowing that this was to be our first romantic memory. Boy, the grandkids will love this story, I would eventually tell her years later. The word *moron* is described in the dictionary as a feeble-minded or stupid person. *Moron* without *Ron* would just be *Mo*, which is what I felt like at the time, Mo of the Three Stooges.

There has always been a practical joker and bit of a prankster as part of my alter ego, so I always love it when I can learn new ways to one-up someone when it comes to gags. Boy, little did I know what I was in for when I met Kim. There are so many funny memories that I have when I think of my life with Kim that I could write a book longer than *War and Peace* filled with our escapades. There was the time she filled the bathtub with ice water, had her makeup-artist brother Neal paint her body with light-blue water-proof body paint, then laid in the tub for an hour right before I got home from work. When I walked in the house I found her on the bed blue and cold, boy, was she a good actress. I freaked out and nearly had ten heart attacks right on the spot, only to discover she really wasn't that great an actress. She started laughing uncontrollably. Man, I was pissed off but only for a few seconds, then I started laughing with her until my sides hurt. I then kissed her, told her that I owed her one and started thinking of devious ways to get her back. Then we had great sex after that but even that was kind of weird and funny because she was still cold and still painted blue, so it was like having intercourse with a moaning talking corpse who kisses back.

When Kim died I didn't know how I was going to handle the enormous task of going on with my life without her. I didn't know whether to move back to Texas, keep our apartment, shoot myself in the head, or start doing heroin, and believe me I considered all four of these options. I frequently asked myself over and over, What do I do now? Where do I go? Who will understand how completely lost I feel? If I had talked to somebody who had just also lost their wife they would not understand what I was going through. And even though they might have been going through the same exact feelings that I was and asking themselves the same questions that I was asking myself, they still wouldn't have understood. Why? Because they didn't lose Kim, I did.

I remember asking myself the question that I had been fearing most of all. How the hell will I ever be happy again? Well, the day after she died, I exercised one of the aforementioned options. I started doing heroin. Let me correct myself, I tried heroin but the experience of falling out of a chair every five minutes, scratch-

When Kim died I didn't know how I was going to handle the enormous task of going on with my life without her.

ing incessantly all over, and craving anything chocolate, was not my cup of tea. That was the first and last time I ever tried heroin. People who have tried it say it is better than sex. Well, to that I say, sorry about your luck, pal, but you're dead wrong! So I can eliminate drugs as an answer to the question of what will keep me happy.

At one time I thought that Kim would keep me happy, but she was taken from me. A few years after Kim died, I started to realize just exactly how true is the saying "It is better to have loved and lost than to have never loved at all." All the material possessions in the world, the Philadelphia Eagles winning the Super Bowl in my lifetime, not even mint chocolate chip ice cream will ever compare to the many fun times I had with the beautiful lady I knew and loved, and the memories I have of my lovely wife Kim. Thinking of her and the way she made me smile and laugh, the wonderful things she taught me and the positive outlook and influence that she still has on my life will always keep me happy.

TIMOTHY HECK

Diapers and Rosebuds

Have you ever stopped to smell
the flowers and truly appreciated
their scent?
I mean *truly*
taken time out of your
day to let the fragrance fill
your nostrils and consume your
taste buds and tickle your pallet
in ways that only a flower can?
I haven't
But

I have taken
the time to wallow
in the unique,
green, foul, nose-wrinkling,
stomach-wrenching, choking,
gagging smell of my
daughter's diaper.
It smells sweeter to me than
all the flowers in the world.
It is the odor of love.

R. L. Love

Circles

My first wife
She was a beautiful
    Blonde-haired
    Blue-eyed . . . you know

I used to wonder until
Was I her Mandingo
    Her Zulu Warrior
    Her Ashanti

I used to wonder until
        Until
        Until . . .

In a crowded BART station I knew
I knew what I was to her
She yelled . . . thirty feet away she yelled
She yelled . . . you black ass fuckin' nigger

She yelled . . . you black ass fuckin' nigger

**ONLY THE DEAD
CAN KILL**

. . . The master's whip awoke again
My father's rope is lashing again
My mother's slap sounded again
Emotions mingled . . . old and new pain pain pain

I was embarrassed . . . not for her or me
But for those who heard
Heard it . . . and believed it
My only self-defense was to walk away

Walking that circle . . . until I kissed her again

Addiction

Addiction is such a demanding lover.

—Ernest Fisher

OLLIS FLAKES

Reflection through Injection

In a period of low-self esteem one endangers one's health
For the brief feeling of contentment while reflecting on self
Without a clue in one's mind of the damage he's doing
Nor does he take care for the life that he was allowed to ruin
As his last bit of contentment is slowly eaten away like a cancer
Without a cure for his problem he seeks for an answer

'N' although he tried but his search was futile
He turned his attention to an IV needle
With its crystalline lag 'n' its crystalline charm
He loaded his gimmick 'n' he stalled his arm
For a brief millisecond he felt the pain
Watching the needle fill with blood as he punctured his vein
Let it drain—let it drain—

He felt this was it
Watching the drug disappear for a registered hit
Upon extracting the syringe the drug took effect in a hazy-like
    dream
As he enters the addictive world of methamphetamine
Stepping towards a mirror to look at his face
Not realizing his movements have quickened in pace
He looks into his own eyes with disbelief and anger
Because the person in front of him looked older and stranger
To himself he thinks, What happened, what did I miss?
Why is my face starting to shrink like this?

*Watching the needle
fill with blood as
he punctured his
vein / Let it drain—
let it drain—*

He doesn't know that his body's reacting to the dehydration
'N' without knowledge of this only raises his growing
   frustrations

Now, that's the least of his problems which'll soon be felt
As his grip on his sanity begins to melt
To give a brief illustration on him methamphetamine psychosis
   destroyed
The awareness of one man rendering him paranoid
Frantically, he searches for voices unknown
Or faces unseen, but he was all alone
For two whole days locked in the clutches of delirium
With nonexisting shadows closing in all around him

Suddenly, the narcotic starts to lose its hold in the chills of the
   night
Day 3 comes along with a feeling of relief in sight
But yet, since he's on a come-down he's feeling worse
Up for three days straight and he is dying of thirst
Awareness slowly seems to come into focus
Along with self-worthlessness, and that feeling of being hopeless
But with some help and a little care, his problem can be set
   straight
By reversing this problem before it's too late
So without further hesitation he breaks his shooting apparatus
With the hopes of never again locking *myself* in a crystal palace.

Michael Fisher

My First Experience

I decided to attend John Casablanca Modeling School. Believe
me, it wasn't because I thought I was all that, because honestly,

It was like the ugly duckling turning into a swan.

to this day even though I feel confident with my looks, I still feel somewhat uncomfortable about them. I really felt that way at age eighteen. So when I paid the $150 entrance fee for this school, trust me, it wasn't because I thought I had the look to be a male model. I was actually paying $150 plus $800 more for six months of confidence classes to basically learn to feel good about myself. Not for the opportunity of seeing myself in magazines or doing fashion shows. But six months and $1,500 later that's exactly what happened.

It was like the ugly duckling turning into a swan. I had learned how to coordinate clothing to what best brought out my features and skin tone. I learned how to take care of my skin. I learned how to walk with confidence and how to walk down a runway. Most importantly, I learned how to express different emotions for the camera. Like any school or talent agency, once you graduate you get automatic job placement. I graduated from John Casablanca on February 8, 1988, and the next day I signed a year contract to be a John Casablanca's model. I signed the contract on impulse, though I never expected to actually get any work.

Three days after signing that contract I was surprised as hell to get a call from my agent (who was a lady named Elaine Arnote). Dillard's department store in Kansas City, Missouri, was looking for a young man for its early spring catalog and Elaine had opted me as one of the five other models the department store wanted. When she told me that, I was absolutely floored. I could not believe that I was about to be doing a photo session and thousands of people were about to see me in print. My first reaction was, my heart started racing like it was going to explode and my hands started sweating. I started to pace back and forth in my small living room. To calm my nerves I lit a Marlboro Red (which I had started smoking only three months earlier) and inhaled deeply. Allowing the strong nicotine smoke to fill my young lungs, I closed my eyes and exhaled a steady, thick stream of smoke while standing absolutely still in the middle of my living room. After all of the smoke was gone, I inhaled deep fresh air and begin to smile again. With a really devilish grin I thought about my parents' reaction when they would see me, their, quote, "faggot failure of a son" in my first print ad. Especially my sister, who thinks that she is so much better looking than the average person.

Thinking about my family immediately made my elation at getting my first modeling assignment crash like a speeding car that smashes into a brick wall at 100 mph. The results were not pretty. In seconds I went from being on top of the world to feeling just like what my parents told me I was, "a faggot failure of a son." I had no one to share this accomplishment with, no friends, no family. It really hurt me to the core of my soul to not have anyone there to share my happiness.

I sat crossed-legged on the floor and started to cry tears of deep pain, tears that I had cried so many times before. Just like the feeling of really wanting to kill myself I had felt so many times before, and again I feel it. What's the sense of accomplishing something if I had no one to share it with? Hell, I didn't even have a pet.

Inside out, I was totally alone. So like I always do, I got up, opened my bottle of Jack Daniels, and guzzled it like it was pure water. The strong amber liquid immediately began to calm my entire body. Before long, like always I was passed out drunk, oblivious to my aching heart and the mellow notes of Mozart.

Fast-forward . . .

Right now, I am standing in a drafty warehouse building with the bright halogen lights glaring in my face. It is hotter than hell under the unmoving glare of this intense light. An agency makeup artist is currently dabbing skin toner along my upper lip so the cut that I have won't show up in any of the photos. The first couple of speedy clicks of his camera somehow loosen me up all the way and I totally forget everything and focus all of my energy on what I was trained to do. My compensation is $1,800 for nine hours of pretty much doing nothing but standing and changing into different clothing. The only bad part of my first modeling experience was having to have my agent take out half. Plus my back, legs, and feet hurt for days. But even though I went through all of that I kept at it and

In seconds I went from being on top of the world to feeling just like what my parents told me I was, "a faggot failure of a son."

If I was making so much money at it, why did I quit, you may be wondering. Well, the reason why is because I crashed into a severe depression where I stayed drunk on Jack Daniels and eventually tried to kill myself.

eventually I built my confidence up to where I wanted it to be. And after my year-long contract with the agency was up I did freelance work and actually made more money working for myself.

If I was making so much money at it, why did I quit, you may be wondering. Well, the reason why is because I crashed into a severe depression where I stayed drunk on Jack Daniels and eventually tried to kill myself. It was Christmas 1993 and I was so miserable and lonely inside and out that I got so shit-faced drunk and tried to kill myself by freezing. In Missouri in the wintertime a person can die in the freezing cold weather. I simply gave up and lost hope on life. My parents and family still wanted nothing to do with me because of my sexuality. And even though I was getting substantial work as a freelance model, I was miserable way to the very core of my soul. So with no winter coat or gloves I went out to a lake in Missouri called Clinton Lake and drank and drank until I couldn't remember anything. All I remember is driving out to the lake in the freezing cold and sitting by the rocks.

When I woke up I was in the hospital with severe frostbite. Luckily I didn't have to have anything cut off. I'm not sure how it happened but I was committed to the crazy ward where I was a guest for two years. When I was finally able to leave I still had my depression but I didn't want to kill myself. At therapy I started on a new hobby. I learned equestrian riding and then learned to jump fences on the horses that I came to love. To this day I would sometimes much rather spend my days around horses than people.

So even though I crashed and burned and never went back to modeling and today I look nothing like I used to look when I was eighteen to twenty-three, I have no shame, embarrassment, or regret over my having been a professional male model. Oh, and it is the biggest thrill in the world to open a magazine or newspaper and find yourself looking right back at you in a suit and tie, tuxedo or something nice. But what is even better are the paychecks. Maybe sometime in the future if I get my shit together I'll go back to modeling. Even though I'm thirty-four, I don't look my age. So I'll do good, even now.

R. L. Love

Falling Twice

I fell deep
I fell hard
I fell slow

Before my falling I sold cocaine
                I sold my car
                I sold my soul

Before my falling I had a hip chick at my side
                Had hip-hop be my groove
                Had hop ease my pain

Finally I had arrived . . . arrived to prison
                Arrived to one hospital after another
                Arrived to play tag with death

Finally I got support from my family
                I got clean for myself
                I got I got I got

It was easy to forget
                To be pompous
                To point at them . . . so I did

And I did . . . until again I fell slow
                I fell hard
                I fell deep . . . again

I fell slow / I fell hard / I fell deep . . . again

Reflection

We act according to the way we see things.

—Gary Harrell

🔲

MICHAEL FRANCIS

Only the Dead Can Kill

A room full of plastic faces with little rubber mouths
With sharp stinging words shot from beneath bushy beating
    brows
Petty power plays made by weak, small-minded, cowardly
    imposters
They, not for a moment, worry about what the ultimate cost is
So many promising lives ruined by their tiny wooden gavel
To taste their idea of justice is like eating gravel
With a dull pain behind the eyes of the victim who suffers
No relief to be given, not even from their own mother
Rejected by a society they never wanted to be a part of
Forced into a prison cell that's as tight as a glove
Now it's inhuman animals they do create in these cattle pens
Where you count no woman or man as your true friend
Battlefields run wild by a greedy authoritarian administration
You learn to live by your wits to your opponents' frustration
To live past the first decade is truly a miracle
To think, your lawyer said that this term was a great deal
'Course he's not the one doing this time in a hellhole
Just to end this torment, you'd sell your very soul
You watch in bitter detachment as you lose your humanity
You'd kill or be killed just to once again feel truly free
Life loses its value to the lowest denominator
You begin to know how it must feel to be the terminator
Feelings and regard for another die oh so quietly in this never-
    ending existence of perpetual midnight

Anger and rage are the only emotions that feel right
Then all at once it hits you, it surely is for true . . . Only the dead
    can kill.
Degradation becomes the norm
As human rights are just a faded memory to scorn
Subjugated to conditions no sane man would accept
Your very humanity you become conditioned to reject
Simple morals are tossed to the wayside
True feelings are now something you learn to hide
All you care for has been stuffed so deep within your mind
They become near impossible for you to find
Life becomes something hard to bear
For all you've ever heard of hell is surely there
And as the light fades slowly from your eyes
Surely you come to realize . . . Only the dead can kill.
You acquire a dead man's stare out of tombstone eyes
You speak to no one 'cause you're tired of all the lies
You hate with a passion that is oh so strong
You care not if you get along
'Cause there's no more value on life
Just suffering and strife
No matter how hard you've tried, all life within you has died
'Cause deep down inside, you know . . . Only the dead can kill.

LONDALE WALTON

Bayside

Extending my legs their full length, resting upon my stool, I gaze out of my family-room windows in search of the peace and tranquility of the San Francisco Bay. Long wide windows open to my view of the world. Outside these glass panes the chaos and madness is forever replaced with sailboats grazing the water tops en route to nowhere. The beautiful landscape is of green hills and salty water that seems to go on forever, stopping only for winding mountain roads that lead to million-dollar homes.

Fortunately, this is my office space as well. This is where I take time out for myself and plenty of writing: journals, various letters and meaningful short stories to my daughter Saoirse. Oftentimes, I sit comfortably, with the idea of she and I outside, playing, laughing, and sitting beside the bay. Daddy's day in the sun with Sao. Cold water at our feet, coursing through our toes, tossing in various shapes of colored pebbles and watching the ripples race towards forever. Picture perfect.

The kitchen is small and simple. No noisy appliances or confusing mechanical toys to figure out. Yet I've seen the same luxuries as most: cooking capabilities, plumbing, and shelves to store my selections. I choose not to cook much. As in other kitchens, the aroma of chicken, beef, or fish will eventually course the nostrils.

With all this luxury at my fingertips, I'm unhappy. In fact, I'm miserable.

Unfortunately, my prime real estate is owned by the state of California. A 5 x 8 San Quentin Prison cell is home: my living quarters, kitchen, bathroom, bedroom, and office space as well.

The peace and tranquility that surrounds the bay is located on the outside of the 150-year-old medieval-looking fortress. The outside. Inside, it's cold and bland. In my reality, I live in chaos. Inmates yelling, obscene gestures and loud remarks all hours of the day. I'm forced to hear the lies and cries of a thousand other innocent victims who are in search of someone, anyone, willing to listen and share the pain of being caged up as animals are. I witness the glazed, bewildered shock of people's lives that have been shattered, as my own. Pain. I hear them. I see them. I know exactly what they're going through. It's something we're unable to share. I see the pain. I know the fear of looking in the mirror and no longer recognizing the person I once was.

I'm forced to hear the lies and cries of a thousand other innocent victims who are in search of someone, anyone, willing to listen and share the pain of being caged up as animals are.

*I really am a two-
parts person.*

PATRICIA ROBINSON

Untitled

I really am a two-parts person. My curious side is definitely from my biological family, and the side of me that will rise from any failure comes from my foster family. I am curious about almost everything. There is always that ever-present *why*.

Make the
Best out of
Everything
So I always
Question myself in good times and especially
In bad times
And in all ways I set my sails,
And full speed
Ahead.
I basically like myself more than
Those might imagine.

DWIGHT YOUNG

If I Had a Chance, What Would I Tell My Mother's Killer Moments before the Murder?

I would say
whatever it was
she did that made
you mad
can you please
forgive her and don't hurt her

because if you could see the
future and view the damage
and see how much hurt
you have caused
you'll probably put down
the knife right now and take
a second to process
your thoughts

so many lives have
been affected
my momma's life wasn't
the only one that was lost
the choice you made
when you took her
away, her family
is who paid that cost

so many questions
I have with no momma
to answer them

can you picture a beautiful
single mother giving birth
to a set of twins
and defending them
by whatever means
doing whatever she
had to do for her young
shelter them comfort them
and prepare them for
the storm

but no that didn't happen
me and my brothers

*my momma's life
wasn't /the only
one that was lost*

**ONLY THE DEAD
CAN KILL**

*I was dealt a bad
hand / since the
day I was born /
and I guess I must /
accept it all*

were deprived of that
and I would gladly
knock on heaven's door
or kick down hell's
gate to get
her back

if only you could
see all the tears
that you have caused
so many
you killed my mother
for whatever reason
and at the same time
crippled her family

you've taken so much
from me they say
everything happens for
a cause
I was dealt a bad hand
since the day I was born
and I guess I must
accept it all

TINA TATE

Tired

Tired of jail
Tired of people thinking they're going to hell
Tired of people tryna use me
Tired of people thinking they can school me

Tired of people tryna do me
Tired of some people ooh wee
Tired of being mad
Tired of being sad
Sometimes I just want to be glad
Tired of portraying to be happy
When the back of my hair is nappy

Tired of portraying to be happy / When the back of my hair is nappy

TINA TATE

If I Were in a Theme Park

If I were in a theme park I'd most definitely be a roller coaster 'cause at times my life is going fast and then it can slow right down. It goes uphill and it goes downhill. Sometimes it goes in circles. For example, as the roller coaster takes off slow, so did my life. Then it sped right up as I became a teen and started disobeying. Then I started going downhill like a roller coaster when I started failing my classes and skipping my classes. Then I started going uphill like a roller coaster. My grades got better and I continued to grow mentally.

Now my life just seems like it's been going in circles. And I say this because I go to jail, get out, and do the same things. It's just a circle, the same circle. My feelings about this are so mixed up. At times I feel good and happy. Then at other times I feel mad and sad. The times I feel good is when I'm getting money and taking care of my loved ones, especially my sister. I feel good when my mom asks for money and I can give it to her. The times when I'm mad and sad is when I come to jail, when I can't get money anymore, and when I can't provide for my family anymore. That's when I get sad and think there could have been another way to do things. At times I think I need to get out. I know I need to get out of the circle but I'm not ready to get out.

At times I think I need to get out. I know I need to get out of the circle but I'm not ready to get out.

I am the dark, chill wind that you feel cuts you to the bone

MICHAEL FRANCIS

Untitled

I am the dark, chill wind that you feel cuts you to the bone
I am that cold gray landscape that November brings
I am that almost-heard whisper that you feel tingle down your
    spine
I am that bump in the night that springs you out of slumber
    like a shot in the dark
I am that nightmare you cannot quite remember when sunrise
    finally dawns
I am that guilty feeling you cannot quite shake
I am what I am because no matter what, you need me.
You need me first to feel alive
Alive in this dead-end existence you clung to so precariously
    in the balance between light and dark
I am that strength derived from that fear you try to hide
I am that numb feeling you get before all hell breaks loose
I am that touch of insanity that saves your life when all else fails
I am what I am because when all's told, you need me.

I am what I am because when all's told, you need me.

DWIGHT YOUNG

Perception

I think I'm perceived
As a decent loving father
A man of many principles with a lot
Of morals and values
I'm also perceived as a miracle

A blessing amongst the youth
Because in my heart and spirit I know
I'm endangered. From my lips
I'm telling you the truth
I bet I'm perceived as
A product which is stamped
Tagged and laid on the shelf
For sale. My price tag
And my serial number
Was given to me the
Day that I landed in jail
I know I'm perceived as
A statistic, a young black
Male who is destined to
Die by genocide. A black
Man's life expectancy in '97 was
Only to the age of twenty-five
Did you perceive my twenty-sixth birthday
I bet you never dreamed of that
It's 2005 coming on 2006, my twenty-seventh birthday
Now picture that!

A black / Man's life expectancy in '97 was / Only to the age of twenty-five / Did you perceive my twenty-sixth birthday

DWIGHT YOUNG

His-tory of Pain Runs Deep

Have you ever felt pain
Not the external, but the
Internal, feel of it
Runs deep
Pain has planted
Itself inside my soul
My bloodline has turned cold

ONLY THE DEAD
CAN KILL

*still the pain / runs
deep / But the boat /
sails on*

But it is a direct flow
For the agony inside to grow
My roots are thick in width and the
Length of it runs deep
Intertwining within the
Four chambers of my heart
Steadily applying pressure
Manifesting itself in every beat killing
My spirit to continue on
The will in me has grown weary
And the shackles around my neck
Hands and wrist are rusted
But remain unbroken so many words
Have been said but the truth remains unspoken
From the blood shed and the tears
Weeped of my history. And still the pain
runs deep
                    But the boat
        sails on

DWIGHT YOUNG

Have You (Ever)

Have you ever desired
Something so bad
But it was just too far from
Your reach

Have you ever wanted to express
Your feelings to someone
But at those moments
You found it very hard to speak

Have you ever wanted to
Hold on to someone
But at the same time
That someone didn't
Want to be held

Have you ever tried
To mend a broken heart
That you knew could never
Be healed

Have you ever
Fell hard over heels
For someone
Just to find out their love for you
Was never true

Have you ever went to sleep
On top of the world
Just to wake up with
The world on top
Of you

Have you ever had the
Feeling that some things in the world
Will never change, or be right

I have

It's a feeling
I've felt
My whole entire
Life

*Have you ever went
to sleep / On top of
the world / Just to
wake up with /
The world on top /
Of you*

MARQUEZ HARRIS

Untitled

To myself I'm a sardonic, a bitterly sarcastic asshole
To others I seem to come off as hilarious
What the hell is wrong with me
Just cuz I don't commit myself seriously to anything
Or the white lies that make up my exterior
Is it the rules I break that I feel make me inferior
Is it the weed I inhale that stalls my mind from thinking
Or the possible threat of a baby that leads me to drinking
All in all I'm slowly sinking, like slow sand . . .

MARQUEZ HARRIS

Untitled

What the hell was I thinking, fucking, smoking, and drinking
Running the streets, like a wolf runs the woods
From city to city, block to block, 'hood to 'hood
I was crazy, or on my way, thank God I was blessed with this day
I played with my life like it was expendable but the key was to
   be dependable
Chasing, indulging in all the things that gratified me instantly
Having girls upon girls, women over women, lying intensively
I always got what I wanted in the end, but I found out karma is
   another name for revenge
I laughed at love like a joke, until I gave my heart and it got
   broke
That was lesson one, something I will surely teach my son
I had my priorities reversed, what I wanted came first
I was so into myself, if I was in a bag of Jolly Ranchers I'd be
   the twelfth

That was lesson number two, the only one who likes you is you
I eventually learned the problem with my life was my thoughts
How I reflected and acted what I'd been taught
The turning point of my life was there, lying, smoking, drinking,
    I had my share
To some the world can be so unfair, and to those I showed I care
Everything happens for a reason, for a greater good, I should
    have been in hell
I never liked matching bracelets, but I realized what saved my
    life was jail.

*I never liked
matching bracelets,
but I realized
what saved my life
was jail.*

Francis Smith

Do You See?

Some say the eyes are the windows
To the soul
When you look in my eyes
Do you feel bold . . . get mesmerized
And try to hold my gaze
Or does the pain you see
Make you catch your breath and turn away?

When you look at my soul
Do you feel whole
Feel more secure in your role . . .
The part you play every day
Every day that you close your eyes
To the realities
Suffered by me and my breed
A holocaust
Right here at home
On these inner-city streets.

ONLY THE DEAD
CAN KILL

When you look in my
eyes / Why do you
gasp . . . / Catch your
breath?

Can you see me
at the age of nine
/ Contemplating
suicide / Drinking
wine at the age
of ten / Are my
eyes dim?

When you look in my eyes
Why do you gasp . . .
Catch your breath?
Do you see the wreckage past . . .
The senseless death of innocence?

When you look at my soul
Does it look withered?
Do you see all the nights I cried
Rivers cold I shivered
Lost all alone
Without a hand to help me home.

So tell me . . . what do you see
Can you see me at the age of three
Running through Tenderloin streets
Surrounded by pimps, bums, junkies, freaks

Can you see me at the age of nine
Contemplating suicide
Drinking wine at the age of ten
Are my eyes dim?

How about eleven, twelve, thirteen
Smoking crack and PCP
Log cabin, YGC

Can you see the man that molested me
Even to this day
The painful price I pay

If you look through my windows
You should pay a toll to see my soul.

I paid
Every single day.

Take a look now
Do you see the anger
All the chaos, constant danger
Who stabbed me five times from behind

Was it a stranger
Or a friend
Can you see the end
Did I lose or will I win?

When you look at my soul
Is it ugly
Is there even a true likeness of me?
Bright blue eyes, crooked smile.

Do you see me as a loving child
A cocaine freak
Do you see the athlete and the geek?

When you look through these windows
To my shoulders do you feel my strength
Or does what you see make you fold
Old, hollow, cold

Can you see the stains and the bruise
Would you wear my worn-down
Tennis shoes.

When you look in my eyes
Do you see my pride
The wealth of love deep inside

Do you understand why I'm free
Why I wear my heart on my sleeve
Go ahead, take a look
My life is an open book

Just remember
Each time you pretend
To turn the page
Take a gaze

See the precious life I saved
Then knock on the door
And stay.

SHADRACH PHILLIPS

Lost between the Cracks

Painful memories, flashes, glimpses of a mind maddening at times, numbing void. This void which I find is so frighteningly easy to get lost within, seems to have no parameters or visible borders.

It is my strength, my refuge, a place of hiding, in times of chaos, situations where I'm overpowered physically, where physical pain is so excruciating that I have to short-circuit myself or change the channel as a self-preservation tactic.

For instance, when I was stabbed in my eye, the knife going in and fracturing my skull, another blow through my front teeth nailing me in my throat, another to my ear, in front of my eight year old brother, blood coming out of every orifice of my head with the exception of my left eye, my biggest thought was, I'm supposed to be the strong one, can't let him see me panic. Missing teeth, warm blood coming out of my eye, nose, ear, and mouth from cracked-out teeth. I knew, and could feel my life creeping out of me.

When I heard him say, "Bro' are you alright?" pain so severe and excruciating it felt as if I was being hit with a sledgehammer as I lay in a bed of coals and flames.

"It's nothing CJ, lock the door," tiny footsteps, and the door locking.

A child complies, dial 911.

A child complies, dial 911.

Every ounce of energy focusing within, a gray colorless calm, then pain remembered, knowing this time death, no fear, strange only li'l brother worries, focus, white flash black glare lair, finally the gray back door, escape this time, windy gray chaos, ah, there, focus.

Show no pain. Focus, paramedics, asking questions, losing concentration about to answer, feeling pain, fuck the question, concentrate gray, back door again, loud windy gray madness, muffled voices, concentrate on gray, no fear, no pain, helicopter sounds, police asking questions, my mother's voice temporarily yanking me back unwillingly through the tunnel or door, anger in response to my mom yelling at me, telling me to tell them who did it, a brief thought of disgust, this is how it ends, huh, I'm dying and she yells at me to rat. Heat and life leaving me, I muster enough strength to remark what the fuck is it gonna change! Escape to my door.

Stress, just how much can we take, if it was weighable, would it be a pound or a key? More than that upon my shoulders, it seems that so much stress rests on my shoulders that, if released, I would rise or float upwards as if I had sprouted wings.

End result when combined a hardened damn near indestructible surface.

Gray uniformed measured squares, lines that appear black from its recesses and shadows, that when you break the coarse gray path down is really nothing but broken-down heated rock and sand. Sand a million pieces of everywhere. End result when combined a hardened damn near indestructible surface. Same as my gray hide-away.

When the sands of a million stressful situations from the brain is combined with a heated blackening heart, refusal to show pain, when it becomes too extreme, I open the door, my retreat becomes a deep abyss, the problem is coming back from this void or abyss.

Concentration so deep, cops in San Jose booking, yanking me this way, that way, my refusal to show or voice pain, hearing my arm break, focus on the void and smile, maddening them more, I smile, a little finger breaks, I smile, yet voice no response, you can hurt and lock up the outside, to an extent. They can't lock up the inside unless you let them, and you can take their induced pain on the outside too if able to focus.

The problem for me is coming back. So inwardly focused, it took me thirty days before I was able to speak properly again. So in essence I welcome this void, but I also fear it. I would like to know more about the crack where I'm able to hide, whose borders hold chaos, euphoria, calm together.

ERNEST FISHER

The First Time

The first time through them gates my stomach was in my throat. I couldn't believe that life has led me to this cold world. We're on this stinking bus all hating life, miserable to the last guy, I thought, but I was wrong. Some of these guys were actually happy to be back, like they were going to Disneyland. I was shocked and amazed what was going on here.

When we first got on the bus we were shackled on hands and feet with our arms chained to a chain around our waist. This was shame, guilt, and total devastation all rolled up in one. We were warned if we talked we would do it only with the guy next to us and if they could hear us they would stop and beat the hell out of us. On top of that, all of our property would be lost on the way there. These guys were bullies with automatic weapons, shotguns and mean dispositions. I had to go to the bathroom and you couldn't go number two but there was a trough for horses and cattle. It was very hard to walk to the back of the bus in shackles, for when any of us headed that way, all of a sudden the bus started swaying, making you fall into other guys that were hating life. They also made sure if you did make it back to the trough, as you were pissing there'd be a jerk on the wheel so you'd pee on yourself, then you'd hear them snicker. This really upset me more than I can tell you. It was humiliation on top of humiliation.

My heart was in my throat. The whole trip. Then my eye fell on San Quentin, a huge ugly cold dirty place. And I was going to be in this place for four years. No God, please, no, I was talking in my head. This isn't happening to me. Please Lord, no. As we move through the gates and they close behind me something in my mind closes also. I have become a rock and no one is going to come into my space. I have shut off the world and life as I knew it.

I have shut off the world and life as I knew it.

We were marched out and the chains were removed. But humiliations were to continue. We were stripped naked where men looked into all my most private spots and orifices, then made to bend over my ass as if I'd put a gun or sharp object up there. Were they crazy? We were thrown orange jumpsuits and mine ran up my ass so far that it knew me better than I know myself. I was in a nightmare world with no end in sight. I was shot up with TB stuff, fingerprinted, photographed, checked for gang tattoos, and asked if I had any enemies in San Quentin. I said none, unless the judge that sent me here was running around in orange.

I noticed some of the guys were reacquainting themselves with old friends, getting smokes, coffee, etc. Then going to a window where my property was gone through, but because I had no money on my books, they took my leather jacket, gold rings and necklace, my boots, and everything I had in the world, a final sign of the predicament I had gotten myself into. I had no one and nothing. Lower than a snake's belly, my whole world crumbled around me. I felt dizzy, hoping this was a sign from God telling me I would be joining him soon. But really my knees were ready to buckle. Then they herded us outside to give us blankets and toilet paper, soap, a toothbrush, and powder. We were assigned bunks in West Block and marched over there.

I was put on the third tier in a cell that was so filthy I wanted to puke. I spent the first three hours cleaning this cell up, just to get moved a half hour after I'd finished, up to the fifth tier. Looking over the rail down this sixty-foot drop made me queasy to my stomach, wondering how many guys were pushed or jumped to their deaths. I was scared of heights and I started to sweat. I kept my back against the bars until the guard opened my cell. Someone's stuff was already in there so I took the empty bunk. Turned out it was a black guy and they didn't mix races in the penitentiary. Maybe they should and maybe that would stop the hate inside but who knows, it might just cause a lot of killing. So here I go again it hasn't even been five hours and I'm on my third move. I'm now moved down to the second tier into a cell with what I found out later to be called a punk named Cherry. A real nice guy but again unhappiness, for Cherry was trying to get her man moved in. I was there overnight. We had a lot of laughs for we knew a lot of the same people in the street. The next day I was moved down the tier into a cell with this old con who loved to sit and talk about old war stories all day long. Cherry came by with some books and s'mores for me. This changed everything, for when I was in a book I was out of this place. I was to read 2,500 books in my eight and a half years of incarceration.

On the first night we had Friday Night at the Improv where people came to their cell doors yelling out their fat-girl jokes, their your-momma's-so-ugly jokes, and for an hour some of the best and worst jokes I've ever heard were told. On Saturday night we had song night with some of the most talented people I've ever heard. There's a lot of talent in the pen, country western, rhythm and blues, soul, rock 'n' roll and once a tenor from the opera who had shot a man for diddling his wife—not to kill him but to make sure the guy never diddled anyone's wife again. The guy lost half his penis and one ball. The judge gave him sixteen months for shooting a firearm inside the city limits.

I learned to send packages and money to a couple of lifers and never again did I go without in the penitentiary when I got them cans of tobacco, all my hygiene and a lighter and jars of Folgers were rushed to me. Plus a small library. I learned quick, and this is good and bad, for I learned a lot of cons and hustles that later got me in trouble, but that's another story.

R. L. LOVE

Empty Victory

Way back in the day
I'd be a certain way
I'd wait like a thief
When someone gave me grief

Patient and waiting, I stood
Blending in the 'hood
Letting the pages turn
As revenge I learn

Slowly I would wait
Vindictiveness is late
No one would find out
Of this I had no doubt

It was no game I played
Because I was betrayed
It was my life I live
In what each pain would give

ONLY THE DEAD
CAN KILL

I'd wait a month, a year
To serve each silent fear
And then the best part
I'd be sitting in the park . . .

and even from my room
I sent impending doom
I sent in silent time
A pain they left behind

Sometimes a house would burn
Or a car couldn't make a turn
Sometimes a wife was hooked
At me they never looked

. . . alone in a cell
I touch my own hell
Whatever did I gain
From serving all that pain

*No face of
satisfaction /
Inside . . . a negative
reaction*

Maybe for a minute
My heart was really in it
But knowing full well
I'm the one who failed

You see I now conceive
My empty victory
No face of satisfaction
Inside . . . a negative reaction

CHRISTOPHER READUS

Yes

I am a young Black man or, as they say today, an African American, who doesn't fit in with his peers. I don't normally fall into the hang-on-the-corner-doing-things-Negro. But I have had this experience, I have tried and done the drink, the 40 oz on the corner, the do-nothing-but-get-high crackhead, the selling dope on the corner. Yes, I've had the empty experience of not being a man.

回

CHRISTOPHER READUS

Mine

So, what is mine?
Today is mine
My life is mine
The disappointments of yesterday are mine
My failed relationships are mine
The decisions that I make are mine
The decisions that brought me here are mine . . .
I come from a loving family, which by the way is mine!
I couldn't have done a better job of picking a mother, father, or
    brother than the one God gave me (which are mine)
The time that I have left to do, before my heart stops beating, is
    mine
Yes, with some of the time that I have left I must spend
    incarcerated
Why I'm incarcerated is not the issue, my crime was against my
    own self
The time I wasted getting high, chasing a dream that I could
    never catch

Why I'm incarcerated is not the issue, my crime was against my own self

The abandonment of my life, my dreams, my job, my
  community, my family
Those experiences also are mine
So I'm paying double because of my bad decisions, which were
  mine.

⊡

LEE WILLIAMS

Roots of My Violence

I learned my violence, most of it, at home, and from the beliefs
that I was taught as a child. Most of it was from innocent people
who were guilty but I believe in my heart they did not know any
better. In the home it was family, and television. Outside the home,
my community.

In the home, first of all, I can't truly remember waking up and
my father living in the house. Other children's fathers were there,
but mine wasn't. I felt different. I was ashamed, separated. For a
while I did not know what or who a father was. Why did I love
a man I didn't even know or who I wasn't sure even existed? He
deserted me. Who am I angry at? Where did this come from? Where
did I fit in? I did not ask to be born. All I knew was my father was
gone.

My mother did her best to raise us with the assistance of AFDC,
church, and my grandmother, who was always there to tell me
along with my mother what a lowdown dirty dog my father was.
They were all the time threatening to whoop my ass. And then
taking a belt or a switch from an apple tree or cherry tree or a lilac
bush and tore my arms, back, and ass up. I remember the welts left
on me. In those days it was normal. So this is how you get a person
to do what you want: beat his ass.

I remember while they beat me they used to say, Do you understand? Well, I did understand. What I understood was, beat them

My mother did her best to raise us with the assistance of AFDC, church, and my grandmother, who was always there to tell me along with my mother what a lowdown dirty dog my father was.

until they understood. Even in fights in the neighborhood you fought until your opponent said, I give up. You had to break them just like I had to be beaten and broke by my family.

I remember my father came to visit us and he bought me and my brother new bikes. We were so happy to get the bikes and we were allowed to ride them in the park across the street. We disobeyed and went farther off into the apartments on another street. My father pulled a branch off a tree and here this man who had never raised me, and my mother and grandmother allowed him to beat my ass, as they put it. Is this the same man they talked about, the lowdown dirty nigger that they called him? Well, he was proud to whoop my ass, and they laughed and said, He's your father and you're to do what he says.

When I was a child, the television carried a lot of violence: Popeye beating Bluto, Mighty Mouse beating the cats, John F. Kennedy, Martin Luther King being assassinated, the Vietnam War, violence was all around me. Things that made me laugh was filled with violence, and things that brought me sorrow was filled with violence. We were constantly fighting each other, and always putting each other down. In my community and in school there were a lot of racial fights, whites against the blacks.

Since I was not happy in the home, I searched for it in school and the street. There I found a different form of violence, drug abuse and alcohol. Narcotics mixed with liquor gave me courage and soothed my inner pain and suffering. Only thing was, I had to keep using over and over again to fulfill the need. This type of violence to myself spread to my environment, family, and all I touched. My life became unmanageable with violence to myself and others.

I was confused and angry at a young age. I remember the name-callings, the quote "You're just like your dad." Ironic, I grew up beating women and jumping from one woman to another, and not taking care of my children just like him.

Reflection

What I understood was, beat them until they understood.

Things that made me laugh was filled with violence, and things that brought me sorrow was filled with violence.

*I'm constantly
seeing some / Of
my ghetto peers
falling victim to the
/ Dangers of the
streets; paralyzed by
cocaine's / Grip.*

BRYAN TROSCLAIR

If Only Tomorrow Was Promised

I very seldom have thoughts
Of brighter days 'cause within the unseen reality
Of these ghetto streets dreams are just
Like wishes, they never seem to come true.
    It's like a grave illusion
Blowing in the midst of hard times and
Never-ending sorrow.
    And nothing seems promised;
Not even destiny's law.
    I'm constantly seeing some
Of my ghetto peers falling victim to the
Dangers of the streets; paralyzed by cocaine's
Grip.
    While death is slowly lurking in
The breeze, killing off all hopes of tomorrow.
    Like today has came and
Went I guess tomorrow will soon be
The same . . . If only tomorrow
Was promised.

BRYAN TROSCLAIR

What If (Echoing in the Wind)

What if there were no
Tomorrows and today was just
A mere memory of the past . . .
    Would my mistakes of
Yesterday cause you to look at
Me with conviction written in

Your eyes then confine me to
Those filthy jails?

What if ghetto life was easy,
If bullets didn't kill and death was only
An illusion . . .
Would the evil wars of these
Ghetto streets still have claimed the
Life of my only friend; then left his
Final words echoing in the wind?

Imagine if silence could
Talk and God couldn't be trusted . . .
Who then would we befriend?
I mean, what if tomorrow
Was promised yet yesterday never
Came . . .
Would most of us still be
Standing here lost and confused?

Even when I'm asleep
I get no relief because my
Reality is more than a dream.
Then the next
Morning when I awake, sometimes
I find myself screaming
In silence wondering why nobody
Never hears my cries . . .
Echoing in the wind.

*Would my mistakes
of / Yesterday cause
you to look at / Me
with conviction
written in / Your
eyes then confine
me to / Those
filthy jails?*

OLLIS FLAKES

Afraid

It's funny how I thought that I would never be afraid of the
  troubles I've caused or the games I played.
Could give a damn about your feelings or how the next person
  felt,
As long as I was the winner of the hand that I dealt.
But now it seems the more that I write, the more I begin to feel,
That when my feelings are expressed then that fear becomes
  real.
This fear came about maybe for the first time.
When I poured out my feelings in ink on the first line.
Damn!
Never knew that my writing could be so strong or so powerful to
  turn my rights into wrong.
To reflect on these insights that were pertaining to me,
Expressions of love, hate, good or bad, or the way that I ought to
  be.
Writing gives me a way to express my fears or the issues,
What I'm stressed about,
Although afraid, it also makes me think, instead of lashing out.

*Although afraid,
it also makes me
think, instead of
lashing out.*

KEITH STEIMLE

What If the Hokeypokey Is What It's All About

As I look back past all the wrong I did
Between now and when I was a kid
Memories flowing like water from a spout
Then it occurs to me, what if the Hokeypokey is what it's all
  about
It is not one but two kinds of dances

Only your age tells if you or the devil prances
There is the hokey bull you have to play
Just to survive another day
Or the pokey sensation of syringe through skin
Which opened the hole to let demons in
But the dance of a child seems innocent
Before all the drugs and money are spent
So I guess it's true in some kind of way
At least for me I can honestly say
The Hokeypokey is what life's all about
And how to switch dancers I'll figure that out

回

KEITH STEIMLE

Things I Think about in Jail

Freedom	Yellow
Syringes	Green
Mushroom clouds	Purple
Biochemical warfare	Orange
Burning bridges	Wheels
Cannabis (my dog)	Gears
Tears	Dreams
Joy	Dragons
Pain	Fire
Bars	Acid
Outer space	Arnold S.
Inner child	Maps
Smiles	Missouri
Light	Mom
Colors	Dad
Red	Friends
Blue	Enemies

**ONLY THE DEAD
CAN KILL**

Cats
Rats
Cars
Energy
Death
Life
School
Magic
Elves
Forests
Guilt
Drugs
Animals
Kids
Normal plans
Spontaneity
Tattoos
Memories
Sun
Moon
Ovens
Gas chamber
Warriors
Slaves
Healers
Prophecies
Philosophies
Goals

Women
Sex
Whore
Wife (love, hate)
Darkness
Caverns
Downward spiral
Drainage
Rainbows
Pools
Gasoline
Matches
Shotguns
Explosions
Water
Boxes
Doors
Locks
Money
Stripes
Power
People
Crosses
Beer
Glass (brown and broken)
Vents
Radiation

MARK YBARRA

What Inspires Me?

I come from a part of society that some consider the have-nots, you know, you probably had some in your schools or, God forbid, on the outskirts of your neighborhoods. The poor family with all the kids dressed in ill-fitting clothes, the what were once bright vivid colors now faded with the many washings, having been passed from the oldest to the youngest or biggest to smallest.

People didn't have to say outright to your face their feelings about your kind, you just knew it. Something about the way their eyes would cross and narrow, their noses wrinkling up as if there were an odor of sewage in the air about you. Well, having experienced that personally, this is what motivates me, to be able to educate myself beyond what they were willing to allow me and putting myself in a place where I am equal if not better in my endeavors than they themselves. It is their disdain of me that motivates me to be the best that I can be, and although there are many people named Mark, there is but one Mark of excellence and, sweetheart, that be me.

People didn't have to say outright to your face their feelings about your kind, you just knew it.

MARGO PERIN

When a Lion Is Chasing You

My mother said we spent six months in Mexico, and one and a half years each in Nassau, Jacksonville, and Miami Beach. But that added up to five years and I was only ten when we moved back to New York, and seven when we'd left. My parents' untruths thickened and a tightrope appeared, separating the world of truth from

the world of lies. I blindly walked this tightrope, never knowing into which abyss I would fall, the one holding the truth or the lies.

Now that we were back in New York, I was to behave as if we had never left. In the last three years my father had been beaten up, my mother had tried to kill herself, my brother had almost died in a car accident, and we'd changed locations five times. But the bounce in my father's step, the Old Spice, and the freshly laundered handkerchief in his breast pocket made it look as if it had all been a dream; a nightmare, not reality.

We took up house on the Upper East Side again, this time on the ninth floor of a shiny white brick apartment building at Seventy-seventh and Lexington. How my father had gone from having no money to pay for my brother's hospital treatment, as he had said, to paying for this swanky apartment was a mystery. I shared a room with Lina and it was so small that there was only room for a bunk bed. I slept on the top and kept forgetting how low the ceiling was so my day usually started with a bang. Next door was the kitchen and, on the other side, an open-plan living and dining room. Farther down the hallway was Ava and Elizabeth's room, with another room for the boys next door. My parents slept in the master bedroom at the back. The apartment was bare and my mother had to go out and buy everything new.

In the early morning, though, before anyone was up, I heard garbage men slamming metal cans into their trucks, and people clicking along the sidewalks far below, and the screeching of cars, and the rumble of air swirling through the narrow passageways between buildings. Even though there was no river out the window, and no bridge across the way, I could smell we were back where we belonged.

The only remnants of our former life were a photograph album and a colorized family portrait that my father had commissioned when I was five. My mother placed this picture of family unity on the wall between my sisters' bedroom and the boys' and it had to be passed on the way to the bathroom. I squinted at it while waiting my turn, trying to remember what life had been like before we'd left. My mother, smiling with blank eyes, sat firmly in the center with, in these pre-Lina days, Tristam on her lap, her white-gloved hands his only support. Max lay at her feet and Elizabeth and I stood at one side of her, with Ava and Lance on the other. My father towered over us all, smiling, black-haired, freshly shaved, looking as if he was proud of the kingdom he had created. Everyone's mouth was open and smiling, happy looking, except for mine, which was flattened into a thin sliver. My eyes gazed piercingly at the photographer, holding this stranger in my grip, as if contact with an outsider would save me from falling into the abyss that lay just over the horizon.

My eyes gazed piercingly at the photographer, holding this stranger in my grip, as if contact with an outsider would save me from falling into the abyss that lay just over the horizon.

"I'll give you one more chance. Did you take the money?" My father's tone was matter-of-fact.

I squirmed in front of him. That night before dinner at the shiny mahogany table, I had snuck into my parents' bedroom to steal the dollar bills they kept hidden in their top drawer. My father had paused at the head of the table during dinner and addressed us all like a judge.

"Someone's been stealing money," he said flatly.

I didn't dare look up, quaking in fear that he would search under my mattress where I'd hidden the stack of bills. I slipped away from the table when no one was looking, stealthily grabbed the money from under my bed and raced down the hallway to my parents' room, just out of sight of the dinner table. After hurling the bills back into the drawer, I went into the bathroom and flushed the toilet a couple of times, then slipped back into my seat, relieved everyone was still eating and fighting, unaware I'd been gone.

At the end of the meal, my father motioned me to follow him to the living room. He removed a cigarette from his gold case, tapped it, and inserted it into a black cigarette holder. He glanced at me every so often as he dragged on the cigarette, seeming to enjoy my terror. He blew smoke rings slowly, circles lazily tracking the space between us. "Have you been taking money?"

"No, Dad." I forced myself to stand perfectly still.

"Don't lie to me. I have a way of knowing." He looked across at me without blinking. I tried to stare unblinkingly back, until I felt his penetrating blue eyes cross through the boundary of my skull and trace the crevices of my brain until he found the memory of my stealing and putting the money back. It wasn't long before I started blubbering my confession.

That night as I lay in bed with a sore head and bruises on my arms, I looked at the ceiling, wondering how he had found out it was me who had taken the money. I was sure he hadn't noticed me leaving the table. It was like he had some strange, mystical power of being everywhere at once.

I was to hold these two realities: we were atheists, and my father was God. The third reality, that my father had stolen from people, and a lot more money than I had, was carefully concealed behind his well-shined image of respectability. He knew: When a lion is chasing you, you're so busy running, you don't look back.

Dress Outs

I have become institutionalized. When I get out I become uncom-fortable with my situation. I expect my circumstances to change instantly.

—Christopher Readus

回

BROTHER LARRY MCCALLUM

What's It Like Outside?

It's beautiful outside, especially when the guards open the doors to go to the recreation yard, air flowing all over you. When I'm released I'm free to roam all over the city, see the drunk people sleeping out in the streets, dirty, stinking, nasty, no money in their pockets, people panhandling for spare change. I used to observe some of them, especially during the winter months when people were freezing cold. Hey, buddy, give me a drink, they all say that. I look at them as though I'm a hawk and they're a meal just waiting to be devoured but it's not like that. It's just amazing how they're deteriorating. All the citizens in the bottom of the Royal Gate bottle love it, probably because there is so much confusion and turmoil outside until the only thing to do if you've got no job is not to suffer.

I've seen suffering outside, loneliness, victims of crimes unre-ported, death, people dying in their sleep and you don't know you're exposed until it's too late. Everything here in jail is outside also, it's not controllable. Some of us end up in jail, some don't. Society sells the things to us people no matter who, what, or where we are: alcohol, tobacco, firearms, drugs of your choice. As long as money currency is established, it can be gotten. People buy anything that's good and in working condition, no matter what it is.

There are no bunks outside for sleeping, it's only cardboard, wind, rain, cold, and misery for some of us. There are some people like myself who love the outside. It's very refreshing. Coldness is the key to survival if your mind, body and soul can accept the sidewalk for what it really is: a cold slab of concrete. You must survive if you're homeless or else you will surely die because it's a cold world outside.

◪

R. L. Love

One Reality

Rain is asking why
Early morning dawn is tickling the sky
Why did I sleep in the park
As I leave with my shopping cart

We roll on down each street
Blue sentinels waiting to meet
To give a bottle or can
And yes I'm still a man

From bottles and cans I learn
People deserve what they earn
It's health or heart attacks
Each container carries the facts

Some like wine to drink
The colors . . . red white or pink
Some like Pepsi or Coke
Slim-Fast is not a joke

Me I work for myself
And more than financial wealth
I'm earning my daily bread
I'm keeping my dignity fed

You must survive if you're homeless or else you will surely die because it's a cold world outside.

So it's more than making some cash
When you see me go through your trash
I'm healthy I'm working I'm free
And this is reality

回

TINA TATE

Two Different Roads I Can Travel

The road that I'm traveling now I think it's the good life, the fast life. I'm not going to sit here and write a lie. I like doing what I'm doing. I get to do what I want to do. I get to buy what I want to buy. I get to eat what I want to eat. I get to work when I want to work. I'm my own boss. I can take care of my sister with no problem, doing what I do.

But I don't cry 'cause it's part of the game that I'm in.

The only part that bothers me is coming to jail. I don't like it. But I don't cry 'cause it's part of the game that I'm in. A li'l time ain't nothing to me. But it hurts the people that love me, more than it hurts me. My li'l sister is so depressed while I'm in here. It really makes me feel bad that I'm hurting them by my actions. But me being me will probably get out and continue my life of crime.

This is what I know, this is what I am. I know all I'm doing is throwing bricks at the penitentiary saying, let me in, in so many ways. But I got to get it, is the way I see it. If I continue this road, I see myself having a lot of nice cars, nice clothes, and a few big houses. But there's always a price to pay in this game. You just never know how much the price is going to be, and when it's going to be. But you do know the price is going to be jail time. And I know it's not going to be li'l months, it's going to be years, and that I don't want.

The other road I can see me going down is the road I was taught as a youngster by my parents. When I was very young, around four or five is when I can remember, my mom used to always send me to school every day. She helped me with my work and she used to always ask me what I wanted to be. When I was about four and five I used to want to be a nurse. Even as I grew up and graduated elementary school, I still wanted to be a nurse. I got good grades in the fourth, fifth, and sixth grade. I stayed on the honor roll.

When I entered junior high school I was still doing fine. I started slipping up as I moved to high school. I used to get in a lot of fights, so my mom thought it would be best for me to move to Sacramento with my dad. I did okay out there, but I was homesick. I moved back with my mom as soon as it was time for high school. I did okay in high school. I managed to keep my grades afloat, so I wouldn't fail. I don't know what really happened. I got what I needed at home. I got food, shelter, and clothes. I didn't have the best of clothes or the worst of clothes. I just wanted to do my own thing. So I started committing crimes to get what I wanted. My mom or dad never cottoned on to it.

I was brought up to respect and do the right thing. My mom always told me to stay in school and you'll get a good job. She used to say, The grass ain't that green right now, but it'll get greener. And when she found out I was doing wrong, she told me, You'll see the grass always ain't greener on the other side.

I didn't listen. I just kept doing my own thing. But I'm very smart, as I think now, I think I should have listened to Mom and Dad and finished school by going to college and getting that nice job to support me how I want to be supported. I could have still have had the nice cars, the nice clothes, and the houses. I even could have taken care of my li'l sister. But I didn't. It's not too late to go to school and get a nice job.

The question is, What will I do? What choice or road will I go? Only time will tell.

回

GEORGE JOHNSON

Get Out

I don't really want to get out. I don't really want to be happy. If I get out I might fail again. Then what'll I do? I almost don't want to try for fear of failing. I don't deserve to be happy. I'm scared to death. I want to overcome my fear. There's only one way I know of to do that. But I really don't want to use that method. I just don't want to go there anymore. But that's my way of self-sabotage. That's one of the few things I know how to do. I'm even pretty good at it. I've had lots of practice. Hell, I'm a pro at it. Just put a positive goal in front of me and watch me mess it up. And don't be the one to tell me what a nice guy I am. Or how smart I am. Or anything good that you see in me. I'll show you how very wrong you are. How could you possibly feel differently than I do about myself? No!

I hate myself because I'm black. I hate myself because I'm gay.

This is how you should feel about me. You can't trust me. I'll steal from you. I'll con you. I'll lie to you. I'll even go so far as to pretend to love you 'til just the right moment when all the pieces are in place to really rip you off. How could I possibly love you when I hate myself? I hate my life. I hate the way I think. I hate myself because I'm black. I hate myself because I'm gay. I hate myself because I hate myself. I hate myself because I'm just like my father. At least that's what I've been told over and over again. And everyone knows what a jerk he was.

R. L. Love

What Changes?

Within periods of incarceration, I have a place; a space where I create what I need to be in order to survive—a space where I fit in—a space in a closed society. The friendships are established and jobs come easily: I hear the whispers, he's a good worker . . . go talk to Love about the law, etc. . . .

When release day comes I feel like something else . . . culture shock sets in . . . no one calls my name to discuss or write about life, law, or love. I'm unemployed, and saddest of all . . . no one is telling me what to do.

No expectations, no responsibilities, no housing, no clothing, no food . . . and lack of demand causes loneliness. A loneliness I've learned to welcome, as a gift or a curse—I really don't know. I only realize that from those combinations I drift from place to place. A family member or an old friend might spare a bed, a couch, a floor for the night; let's face it, no money makes no comfort (at least that's the way it is for me). From institutionalized structure to nothing but low self-esteem.

Drugs and alcohol; they usually come later. Why? Perhaps it's comfort. Perhaps it's false courage. Perhaps to forget I'm a father. Perhaps so I won't smell myself, see my dirty clothing, or view my filthy tennis shoes. Perhaps even, it's ancient karma . . . perhaps to hide from life, from love, from hope; even from myself.

So I turn my back on a society that is so self-absorbed to carelessly believe incarceration should be enough to help me change course. The lack of patience, among other aspects, keeps me from the homeless shelters, the free clothing, the meal lines, etc. I'm only brave enough to be stupid, knowing my way doesn't manifest a place in free society. Maybe I'm only patient enough, brave enough, to play at death's door, and yet I cling to this other side. It's like having two ideas that still make one dream.

From institutionalized structure to nothing but low self-esteem.

*His home has long
been gone and
his friends are
merely shadows
from his past.*

BRIAN RIGGS

What the Future May Hold

A thick fog of uncertainty manifests around his head as he takes a timid step into a world he once knew in another life. This place had once threatened to diminish his sanity and steal his soul, yet this does not stop him from inching closer to a destiny he is anything but sure of. His mannerisms have changed dramatically and he's not sure if the evils of the insidious city can recognize him anymore. The place he called home harbors every temptation known to man and he is not certain he can face them successfully, but giving up before he has tried is out of the question. The enemy line has been breached, and from here on out his moves must be smooth and calculated if he is to survive the cold city. Behind the bars of captivity his plan of action was honed to perfection, but it seems insignificant now that he is faced with the sudden reality of his predicament. His home has long been gone and his friends are merely shadows from his past. His unscrupulous deeds from his prior life have alienated him from his family and any allies that may have been in a position to help him. So it is on his own that he must press forward and he does this with the defiant swagger of a man that is no longer afraid because he has nothing to lose.

The attack is swift and sudden as he is bombarded by glowing neon liquor store fronts that act as guided missiles to deter him from his destination. He hesitates briefly and the anxiety is coming close to overwhelming him and destroying his progress. A lone icy trail of sweat falls from the tip of his nose and he is frozen briefly in the glowing, hypnotizing light . . .

回

CREDITS

Wilfredo Aguilar © 2005

Edwin Armando Alvarez © 2005

Janice Armstrong © 2005

Brian Baird © 2005

Billy Booker © 2005

Leonard Boyland © 2005

Jasmine Bryant © 2005

Greg Carter © 2005

Aja Cayetano © 2005

Zakiya Craig © 2005

Mecca Femme © 2005

Ernest Fisher © 2005

Michael Fisher © 2005

Ollis Flakes © 2005

Darnell Ford © 2005

Michael Francis © 2005

David Garner © 2005

David Green © 2005

Afrom Hagos © 2005

Mark Hall © 2005

Dwight Hammond © 2005

Gary Harrell © 2005

Marquez Harris © 2005

Roger Hazelett © 2005

Timothy Heck © 2005

George Johnson © 2005

Stephen Logan © 2005

Chaz Long © 2005

R. L. Love © 2005

Dylan M. © 2005

Brother Larry McCallum © 2005

Kristian Marine © 2005

John Martel aka Indio © 2005

Andre Maximilian © 2005

Ruth Morgan © 2005

Randy Nichols © 2005

Christina Passmore © 2005

Michael Payton © 2005

Margo Perin © 2005

Shadrach Phillips © 2005

Thane Pouncy © 2005

Christopher Readus © 2005

Nestor Reyes © 2005

Sean Reynolds © 2005

Brian Riggs © 2005

Patricia Robinson © 2005

Tim Rodrigues © 2005

Michael Rothstein © 2005

Ron Salkin © 2005

Timothy Scott © 2005

Wesley Simms © 2005

Francis Smith © 2005

Latasha Smith © 2005

Keith Steimle © 2005

Tina Tate © 2005

Sharon Thomas © 2005

John Tonini © 2005

Bryan Trosclair © 2005

Deborah Walton © 2005

Londale (Dale) Walton © 2005

Lee Williams © 2005

Kimberley Wright © 2005

Mark Ybarra © 2005

Dwight Young © 2005

About the Contributing Editor

Margo Perin has been writer-in-residence at San Francisco County Jail since 2001. Her anthology *How I Learned to Cook and Other Writings on Complex Mother-Daughter Relationships* (Tarcher/Penguin 2004) was featured on National Public Radio's *Talk of the Nation,* KPFA's *Morning Show,* KALW's *Book Talk,* and KRON 4 TV's *Weekend Edition* and, among other publications, the *Washington Post* and the *Dallas Morning News.*

A Pushcart nominee, she has won awards for her fiction and nonfiction. Her work has been published in the United States and Great Britain, filmed, theatrically produced, and broadcast. She teaches writing workshops in the United States and abroad and can be contacted at www.margoperin.com.

About Community Works

Community Works/West (CW/W) seeks to provide disenfranchised populations in the San Francisco Bay Area with opportunities to build community and give voice to their experiences. CW/W believes that the arts and education can serve as valuable platforms for achieving this goal, incorporating personal expression, alliance-building, and public engagement. CW/W is particularly concerned with the effects of soaring incarceration rates on communities, impacting not only the offending individuals but also families, neighbors, and survivors of crime. CW/W links up with the institutions that most affect our constituents' lives, including the criminal and juvenile justice systems, the public school system, and other community-based organizations, in order to provide enriching, sustainable programs that work to bring communities together. For more information about CW/W programs, call 510.845.3332 or visit us at www.community-works-ca.org.